GOODS TRAFFIC OF TH
LNER

GOODS TRAFFIC OF THE LNER

BY GEOFF GOSLIN

ISBN 1 874103 74 7

J11 No. 64420 at South Lynn on 1st August 1953. GRESLEY SOCIETY

Title page: *No. 5472 with an Annesley to Woodford coal train at Willoughby.* H. E. SIMMONS

Designed by Paul Karau
Printed by Amadeus Press, Cleckheaton

Published by
WILD SWAN PUBLICATIONS LTD.
1-3 Hagbourne Road, Didcot, Oxon, OX11 8DP

LENS OF SUTTON

CONTENTS

This picture of ex-North Eastern locomotives in evidence on Great Central section goods trains in the early 1940s, shows B16 No. 2365 heading a down train and Q5 No. 1274 waiting with an up train in the loop.
A. W. V. MACE/MILEPOST 92½

PREFACE

The change from railways to roads for the general carriage of goods in Great Britain gathered pace in the late 1950s and was virtually complete within 15 years. With the passage of time it is easy to forget the prominence of goods traffic and its economic importance in the days when railways were able genuinely to pay their way. The traffic receipts of the LNER for a typical week in September 1935 are shown below. It will be seen that the proportion derived from goods traffic approached two-thirds of the total.

1935 – Week 38

	Receipts £	*£ per route mile*	*% of total*
Passenger	331,000	52.24	37.87
Merchandise	324,000	51.14	37.07
Coal/Coke	219,000	34.56	25.06
Total goods	543,000	85.70	62.13
Total Receipts	874,000	137.94	

Another illustration of the preponderance of goods traffic can be found in the rolling stock returns. At the end of 1930, the LNER possessed 13,449 carriages, 7,133 other coaching vehicles and 273,050 goods vehicles. This represented one LNER goods vehicle for about every 160 of the entire population of Great Britain. The complete goods stock of the four main groups, plus the ubiquitous private owner wagons, provided a goods vehicle for about every 40 heads of the population. This ratio might be quoted as exemplifying the complete dependency of the commerce of the day on rail transport. It could also be used to demonstrate a low utilisation of the wagon stock. The ordinary goods wagon was highly standardised, long-lived and cheap to build and maintain. Wagon costs might, therefore, be thought to have provided comparatively little incentive to improve utilisation. But financial stringency had led to the curtailment of the LNER's wagon building programme in both 1929 and 1934 and in those years there were insufficient wagons to meet immediate needs. With such an enormous stock it is not surprising that some vehicles actually went missing. In 1925, 367 wagons not seen since 1913 were written off. In subsequent years, wagons not seen for ten years were written off.

Much has been written about passenger services and the general pattern of their operation can readily be deduced from public timetables. Less has appeared on the operation of goods services. Although the various classes of goods locomotives are well known, the uses to which they were put has received little attention. The goods services on some typical LNER routes are described in Chapters 2 to 9. The coverage of a system which required 4,000 goods and shunting locomotives and a quarter of a million wagons is necessarily selective rather than comprehensive. Nevertheless, it is hoped that the chapters which follow will give a fair impression of the variety and extent of the goods services of the LNER and their practical operation.

Some of the following chapters first appeared as articles in *The Gresley Observer*, the journal of the Gresley Society. I am indebted to Dr Peter Rodgers, Hon. Editor of *The Gresley Observer* for permission to publish these articles in suitably amended form.

My thanks are due to Peter Holmes and the late Eric Neve who have provided invaluable help and information throughout. I am also indebted to Ron Woodcock and the late Ken Wildey for information which clarified some otherwise obscure details.

ABBREVIATIONS

CME	Chief Mechanical Engineer	MR	Midland Railway
GCR	Great Central Railway	NBR	North British Railway
GER	Great Eastern Railway	NER	North Eastern Railway
GNR	Great Northern Railway	ROD	Railway Operating Division of the Royal Engineers
GWR	Great Western Railway		
LNWR	London & North Western Railway	WD	War Department
LT&S	London, Tilbury and Southend (Railway)	WTT	Working Time Table

D41 No. 6820 with an up goods train at Kintore on the Great North of Scotland section. The GNSR did not possess any 0–6–0s and employed 4–4–0s on goods traffic. S. H. FREESE

CHAPTER ONE

A BRIEF SURVEY OF LNER GOODS LOCOMOTIVES

THE LNER was fortunate in the quality of its initial stock of goods locomotives. There had been over eight years of war and recovery before grouping. During that period the constituent companies had concentrated their locomotive development on goods rather than passenger designs, hence there was a fair proportion of up-to-date classes in the total taken over. This survey covers the more modern of the pre-grouping designs together with the types introduced by the LNER. In *Table 1* the principal classes are listed with the characteristics that were most important to the operator.

Route availability was one factor in the allocation of motive power. Towards the end of its existence the LNER introduced a system of grading routes according to their civil engineering standards. RA (Route Availability) Numbers 1 to 9 were allocated, 1 representing the most restricted routes and 9 the unrestricted main lines. Most of the lines covered in succeeding chapters were RA9, but Nottingham to Grantham was RA8, and the GN and LNW Joint line was RA7 north of Melton Mowbray and RA5 to the south. The Great Eastern section lines through Ely and St Ives were RA7. Locomotive classes were matched to routes by allocating similar numbers, based largely on axle loading. Although the RA system was not introduced until 1947, it grew out of wartime regulations for the use of engines on unfamiliar routes and the previous ad hoc restrictions which had always been applied to the heavier classes.

From the start there was an operational viewpoint present in the formation of LNER locomotive policy. On 9th February 1923, Sir Vincent Raven, ex-CME of the NER, in his capacity as Technical Adviser to the LNER, presented a report on the organisation of the Mechanical Engineering Department. The report recommended that the Chief Mechanical Engineer, as yet unappointed, should not have control of locomotive running. Instead this should be the responsibility of a Locomotive Running Superintendent in each area, reporting to the appropriate Divisional General Manager. On 22nd February 1923, the Locomotive Committee recorded the appointment of H. N. Gresley (later Sir Nigel Gresley) as Chief Mechanical Engineer at a salary of £4,500 per annum. The first Locomotive Running Superintendent for the Southern Area was W. G. P. Maclure, an ex-GCR man, who attended many of the meetings of the Locomotive Committee. His influence can be detected in various preferences for GCR designs in the early years. The annual locomotive building programme for 1925 and subsequent years was also discussed by the Joint Locomotive and Traffic Committee.

From, the operator's point of view the stock of goods locomotives could be roughly divided into classes suitable for general purpose, mineral and express goods work. The general purpose category was almost entirely represented by 0-6-0s, an exception being the Great North of Scotland which used 4-4-0s for all its main

TABLE 1: PRINCIPAL CLASSES OF LNER LOCOMOTIVES USED FOR GOODS TRAFFIC

Type	*Class*	*Origin*	*Coupled Wheel Diameter*	*Grate Area sq.ft*	*Tractive Effort lbs*	*Max Axle Load*	*Adhesive Weight*	*Wheelbase Engine & Tender*	*RA*
0-6-0	J6	GNR	5′ 2″	19	21,875	18t 0c	50t 10c	38′ 10″	5
	J11	GCR	5′ 2″	19	21,959	18t 0c	52t 2c	39′ 6½″	5
	J20	GER	4′ 11″	26.5	29,044	18t 16c	54t 15c	40′ 11″	5
	J27	NER	4′ 7¼″	20	24,642	17t 18c	49t 10c	38′ 9¾″	5
	J37	NBR	5′ 0″	19.8	25,211	20t 6c	54t 14c	40′ 0″	8
	J39	LNER	5′ 2″	26	25,664	19t 13c	57t 15c	40′ 5¼″	6
0-8-0	Q6	NER	4′ 7¼″	23	28,800	17t 12c	65t 18c	42′ 7¾″	6
	Q7	NER	4′ 7¼″	27	36,953	19t 0t	71t 12c	44′ 4″	7
2-8-0	O1/O3	GNR	4′ 8″	27.5	33.736	17t 12c	67t 8c	51′ 4¼″	6
	O1 Std	LNER	4′ 8″	27.9	35,518	17T 0c	65t 17c	51′ 2½″	6
	O2	GNR	4′ 8″	27.5	36,470	17T 12c	67t 7c	52′ 2¼″	6
	O4	GCR	4′ 8″	26.24	31,236	17t 1c	66t 4c	51′ 2½″	6
	O7	WD	4′ 8½″	28.6	34,215	15t 12c	61t 5c	53′ 1¾″	6
2-8-2	P1	LNER	5′ 2″	41.25	38,500*	18t 13c	71t 10c	59′ 8″	7
4-4-0	D15	GER	7′ 0″	21.6	17.096	17t 16c	34t 12c	43′ 8″	5
	D34	NBR	6′ 0″	21.13	22,100	19t 2c	37t 3c	46′ 8½″	6
4-6-0	B7	GCR	5′ 8″	26	29,952	19t 10c	58t 10c	52′ 9½″	7
	B16	NER	5′ 8″	27	30,031	20t 0c	58t 14c	52′ 6″	7
2-6-0	K2	GNR	5′ 8″	24	23,400	18t 16c	53t 18c	47′ 7½″	5
	K3	GNR	5′ 8″	28	30,031	20t 0c	60t 0c	49′ 1″	8
2-6-2	V2	LNER	6′ 2″	41.25	33,730	22t 0c	65t 12c	56′ 2¼″	9

*Increased to 47,000 lb with booster in use.

Left: *J3 No. 4140 (3306 pre-1946) on ballast duty at Potters Bar on 14th July 1946. Notice the post for a warning board stowed on the front buffer beam.* Right: *J11 No. 6006 on Neasden shed on 9th October 1937.* D. A. DANT and G. T. STAMP

The final development of the Great Eastern goods engine, J20 No. 1289 (LNER 8289) in Great Eastern grey livery at Stratford in 1923. AUTHOR'S COLLECTION

No. 1457 was an early example of Class J39. Seen here on the North Eastern section, it entered service in 1926. PHOTOMATIC

J6 No. 3606 with a down goods at Buxford North Junction. The connection from the one-time Lancashire, Derbyshire & East Coast Railway is seen converging from the right. E. R. MORTEN

requirements. This was an early application of the principle that ideally any locomotive should be capable of handling any train. The use of 4-4-0s with limited adhesion is, however, surprising on a line with many steep, albeit short, gradients.

The GER and NBR built nothing larger than 0-6-0s for goods traffic if the solitary GER 0-8-0 rebuilt from the Decapod is neglected. On both these railways the large superheated 0-6-0 was eventually developed for mineral use to its practical limit with classes J20 and J37 respectively. (Throughout this survey, the better known LNER classifications are used, whether referring to classes in pre- or post-grouping times.) The distinction between general purpose and mineral use was therefore one of age and size rather than of wheel arrangement. To some extent this applied also to the NER where, despite a large stock of 0-8-0s, the later built 0-6-0s of class J27 found much employment on the shorter distance mineral duties. The GNR handed over 110 J6 0-6-0s, a versatile class which served the LNER well and remained intact in British Railways until 1955. Likewise, none of the 175 engines from the GCR of Class J11 were withdrawn until 1954. In the early 1940s a proposal existed to build modernised J11s as an LNER standard type.

The older and less capable pre-grouping 0-6-0s were gradually weeded out by the LNER. Of the total of 2,527 0-6-0s of thirty-seven classes taken over on 1st January 1923, only 1,505 of twenty classes remained by 31st December 1938. In replacement, 316 0-6-0s were added to stock during the period, including ten engines

GCR 0–8–0 Class 8A No. 67. After grouping this engine became LNER Q4 No. 5067 and was converted into a Q1 0–8–0T in September 1944.
AUTHOR'S COLLECTION

Class O4 No. 6286 seen on the North British section. It was built in 1919 as ROD No. 2112 and entered LNER service in August 1924.
AUTHOR'S COLLECTION

Ex-NER 0–8–0 No. 661. The original LNER classification was Q5 but it is seen as fitted with a boiler from a withdrawn Hull & Barnsley 0–8–0 in July 1933 and re-classified as Q5/2.
COLLING TURNER

NER Class T2 (LNER Q6) No. 2274 in Armstrong Whitworth's yard at Newcastle awaiting delivery on 10th May 1920.
LCGB/KEN NUNN COLLECTION

The first Gresley three-cylinder locomotive, GNR O2 No. 461, in grey livery at New England as new in 1918.
F. W. GOSLIN

J38 No. 65919 with a train of Midlothian coal destined for shipping from Fife, seen here leaving the Forth Bridge at North Queensferry on 5th June 1951. E. D. BRUTON

taken over from the Midland and Great Northern Joint Railway in 1937. The remaining 306 comprised 271 J39s and 35 closely similar J38s. Both classes were introduced in 1926. Although they were nominally Gresley designs they followed Darlington rather than Doncaster traditions. The J38s, with 4ft 8in diameter wheels, were basically mineral engines and were used on ex-NBR lines throughout their lives. The J39s, with 5ft 2in wheels, were widely distributed as general purpose locomotives. A last batch of eighteen J39s, ordered after the outbreak of war, entered services in 1941. Both classes remained intact until 1959 and the last J38s were not withdrawn until 1967.

The large number of NER 0-8-0s has already been mentioned. Class Q5 had been introduced in 1901. The ninety Q5s were followed by a superheated version, Class Q6, of which 120 were built.

The final development was the 3-cylinder Q7 design. Of the fifteen Q7s, ten were completed after grouping. Their haulage capability was well used in the iron ore trains worked over arduous gradients from Tyne Dock to Consett. On the GNR, Gresley had introduced the 2-cylinder 2-8-0s of Class O1 in 1913. Twenty had been built by 1919. In 1918 a solitary 3-cylinder 2-8-0, No. 461, of Class O2 was built, followed in 1921 by ten more with a revised layout of cylinders and valve gear. Another fifteen entered service in 1923/4. It was intended to build fifty O2s under the 1924 building programme but these were cancelled in November 1923. By then the ex-ROD 2-8-0s of Class O4 were becoming available and there is little doubt that the economic advantage of purchasing the ex-ROD engines led to the cancellation of the O2s.

Two early ventures by the LNER into the realm of very large goods locomotives were present at the Railway Centenary Exhibition at Darlington in 1925. The Class U1 2-8-0 + 0-8-2 Garratt was intended solely for banking purposes on the Worsborough incline. This bank, 3½ miles of 1 in 40, including the two Silkstone tunnels, was

Class O1 No. 3467 at Doncaster shed. AUTHOR'S COLLECTION

situated on the route used by coal trains from Wath concentration yard via Penistone and Woodhead to the Manchester district. Throughout the long climb to Dunford Bridge a Class O4 2-8-0 and banker would take 66 wagons. The Worsborough incline required two additional O4s, making three bankers in all. The GCR had prepared schemes to replace the Worsborough bankers by Garratts, one of which would do the work of two O4s. In October 1923 the LNER Locomotive Committee considered a proposal for two Garratts at a total cost of £20,000. In April 1924 one such locomotive was ordered from Beyer Peacock at a cost of £14,395. Three months later, Gresley obtained approval for a change from 2-cylinder to 3-cylinder units at each end, at an additional cost of £500. The wheel spacing, previously based on the O4 design, was altered between the first and second coupled wheels to enable Class O2 motion parts to be used. The Garratt duly did the work of two O4s and halved the number of enginemen required. A single fireman, however, had to fire a grate of 56.5 sq.ft., the largest ever used in Great Britain.

The Class U1 Garratt No. 2395 when new on a trial trip up the line to Woodhead. REAL PHOTOGRAPHS

The Garratt No. 2395 and an O4 banking in tandem on the Worsborough incline. SCOTTISH RAILWAY PRESERVATION SOCIETY

A wartime view of P1 No. 2393 heading an up coal train at Hadley Wood on 24th July 1941. A. R. GOULT

The other new locomotive shown at Darlington was the first of the two Class P1 2-8-2s. These engines were authorised at a cost of £8,000 each in August 1923. Those were heady days with the newly formed LNER achieving levels of traffic and revenue which were never repeated. It has become traditional to write of the introduction of the P1s as a failure due to operating restrictions on the 100-wagon coal trains which they were set to work between New England, Peterborough, and Ferme Park, London. It will be shown in Chapter 2 that the restrictions eventually became minimal and no doubt could have been removed altogether if it had been desired to work such trains in any numbers. As it was, operational development of that particular traffic was concentrated on the introduction of lighter and faster trains which enabled New England crews to work up to Ferme Park and back again in a single shift. The P1s had much in common with the early Gresley Pacifics. By 1938, 114 Pacifics were at work, largely on duties at one time operated by smaller locomotives. There is reason to believe that a somewhat similar situation would have pertained with the P1s had it not been for the ready availability of the ex ROD 2-8-0s as described below. Many years later, the British Railways 9F 2-10-0s, originally conceived as 2-8-2s, were widely used on ex-LNER lines performing a variety of duties ranging from mineral traffic to express goods workings. There is a very close similarity between the basic dimensions of the P1 and 9F designs. The P1s were originally fitted with boosters but, despite the success of the system in the USA, the application on the P1s seems to have been attended with difficulties and they were eventually removed.

The availability at low cost of the surplus ex-ROD 2-8-0s had a controlling effect on LNER policy for the provision of mineral locomotives. The engines had been built to a GCR design (LNER Class O4) in the later stages of the 1914–1918 war. No less than 273 of these locomotives were purchased in three batches. To these must be added another 131 of the same design taken over from the GCR and 17 fitted by the GCR with larger boilers and classified O5 by the LNER. The O5s were gradually rebuilt as O4s, making a single class of 421 engines. As early as 1st November 1923 the Locomotive Committee agreed to include 125 ex-ROD O4s in the 1924 building programme, to be purchased and reconditioned at a cost not exceeding £3,500 each. The major item of the reconditioning was the provision of copper fireboxes in place of steel. The purchase price was £2,000 each and in 1926 it was recorded that the total cost of the batch was £423,239, equivalent to £3,386 each.

The next batch of 48 locomotives was offered in 1925 by the Cohen Armstrong Disposal Corporation at £1,800 each. B. A. Firth, Chairman of the Locomotive Committee, negotiated a reduction to £1,500. New fireboxes and reconditioning brought the total cost to £2,741 each. Finally, in 1927, 100 engines were purchased from the Government Disposals Board. In the year following the coal strike, and with the LNER as the only likely bulk purchaser, there was a buyer's market. Firth and the Deputy Chairman, Lord Faringdon, negotiated a purchase price of only £340 each. With the deterioration due to two extra years of storage to make good, the reconditioning cost might well have been greater than that for the previous batch but it is probable that it cost the LNER no more than £2,000 each to purchase and put the engines on the road.

The total cost of purchases and the reconditioning of the 273 locomotives was approximately £750,000, about half the cost of equivalent new building at contemporary prices. Finally, in 1927, Gresley reported to the Locomotive Committee that he had purchased from the Surplus Stores Liquidation Department their whole stock of spares for the ROD locomotives, comprising 326 tons of ferrous and 36 tons of non-ferrous items, at £3,600 free on truck at depot. The price paid was only slightly above the scrap value. Gresley claimed that nearly all the spares would be used to maintain the 467 locomotives of the 2-8-0 type belonging to the company. This was an example of the manipulation of figures to impress the Committee – 46 of the total of 467 were O1s and O2s, for which the spares would be of no use.

The addition of 273 O4s rang the death knell for various classes which might otherwise have a longer life. These included the entire ex-GNR fleet of Ivatt 0-8-0s and 0-8-2Ts, and the fifteen ex-Hull and Barnsley 0-8-0s of Class Q10. The latter were all withdrawn in a six-month period in 1931. Some ex-Q10 boilers were re-used on Q5 0-8-0s, the variant being classified Q5/2. Later, in 1936, Gresley proposed the withdrawal of ten ex-GCR Class Q4 0-8-0s as they were '*deficient in haulage power with 25,000 lb tractive effort and a coal consumption of 70 lb/mile compared with a more modern type of 31,000 lb tractive effort and a coal consumption of 65 lb/mile*'. The comparison was apparently between the saturated Q4s with slide valves and the O4s. In the event, only six saturated Q4s were withdrawn before the advent of war caused the plans to be revised.

The acquisition of the ex-ROD 2-8-0s enabled loading to be increased on various workings which previously had seen nothing larger than 0-6-0s. On coal trains from Whitemoor to the Temple Mills yard at Stratford the O4s took sixty wagons against fifty for ex-GER J17 or J19 0-6-0s or fifty-five for J20s. The NBR had long been considering larger engines for the Thornton to Aberdeen

Ex-Hull & Barnsley Q10 No. 2509. Withdrawn in October 1931, it bequeathed its boiler to a Q5 and its number to Silver Link. COLLECTION L. R. PETERS

O4 No. 6252 with an up coal train at Willoughby in August 1938. H. E. SIMMONS

coal trains. The O4s at last satisfied the requirement, taking forty wagons compared with a maximum of thirty for a J37.

After the P1s of 1925, no new mineral or heavy goods engines were built until 1932 when eight O2s entered service. They were based at March and worked coal trains from Whitemoor to the Temple Mills yard at Stratford. Twenty-five more O2s were built in 1942/43, after which wartime demands were met largely by loans. A total of 211 American-built 2-8-0s were on loan from the United States army in the 1942/5 period, together, in 1943/47, with sixty LMS-type Stanier 2-8-0s which had been built at Doncaster and Darlington. Sixty-eight of the Stanier 2-8-0s, Brighton and Darlington-built,

US Army class S160 2–8–0 No. 1833 taking water at Leicester Central when working an up goods train. AUTHOR'S COLLECTION

Class O6 No. 3518, a Stanier 2–8–0 built for the LNER at Brighton as No. 7669 in 1944. Renumbered 3118 in 1946, it is seen at York on 11th August 1947 after a second renumbering in the previous February. Two months after the photograph was taken, it was transferred to the LMS, becoming their No. 8723. After nationalisation it received its fifth and final number, 48723, which it carried until withdrawal in August 1968. PHOTOMATIC

WD 2–8–0 No. 78673 with an up goods at Potters Bar about to be overtaken by the 10.34 a.m. Leeds to King's Cross on 24th July 1946. No. 78673 was purchased by the LNER, becoming O7 No. 3153 and eventually BR No. 90474.
LCGB/KEN NUNN COLLECTION

Thompson O1 No. 3796 with an up Class C goods train at Staverton Road, south of Rugby, in 1946. J. A. G. H. COLTAS

were taken into LNER stock in 1944/46 as Class O6. Their advent, unannounced, in LNER livery caused contemporary observers much surprise and speculation. They were all transferred to the LMS in 1947 with the exception of one laggard which went to the London Midland Region in the first month of 1948. The Ministry of Supply Austerity 2-8-0s were much the longest serving of the types loaned in wartime. Large numbers worked on the LNER from 1943 onwards. In 1946/47 two hundred were purchased to become Class O7. They gave good service to British Railways on ex-LNER lines, becoming, for instance, the main motive power for the New England to Ferme Park coal trains until the advent of the 9F 2-10-0s.

In 1941 Edward Thompson became CME after Gresley's death. Thompon's standardisation proposals included a 2-8-0 rebuild of the O4 design. The first engine appeared in 1944 as Class O1, the ex-GNR 2 cylinder 2-8-0s being reclassified as O3. To some extent history repeated itself. The availability of Austerity O7s built for the Government reduced the requirement for O1s and only 58 were put into service compared with 410 general purpose 4-6-0s of Class B1.

The NBR and GER, in addition to lacking eight-coupled engines, both relied on 4-4-0s for express goods work. The NBR built a series of mixed traffic 4-4-0s with coupled wheels of 6ft 0in diameter, in each case the equivalent of an express passenger type with 6ft 6in wheels. The final development was Class D34, the 'Glens'. They achieved a magnificent reputation on the West Highland line, but, however good the design, there was no comparison in size with the mixed traffic engines of the NER, GCR and GNR. Among its small locomotives, the GER possessed some very useful intermediate 2-4-0s with 5ft 8in coupled wheels, LNER Class E4. In the next generation of designs there was nothing between the 0-6-0s with wheels of 4ft 11in diameter and the 'Claud Hamilton' series of 7ft 0in 4-4-0s. Vacuum fitted engines were necessary for the express goods trains which ran north from London Spitalfields over the GN/GE Joint line. At grouping, there were twenty-seven Clauds with vacuum ejectors

B7 No. 5465 working an up Class B goods train at Willoughby in August 1938. H. E. SIMMONS

available for use on these trains, possibly a unique instance of engines with wheels as large as 7ft 0in diameter being specifically equipped for goods work. The LNER soon drafted ex-GNR K2 2-6-0s on the joint line express goods, enabling the loads to be increased from 25 to 40 wagons.

The NER, GCR and GNR, all operating long-distance vacuum-fitted goods trains, had put new designs of mixed traffic engines into service shortly before grouping. Twenty-eight of the GCR engines, Robinson 4-6-0s of Class B7, were handed over to the LNER, and a further ten, already ordered by the GCR, were built in 1923/4. The NER built the first of their 3-cylinder 4-6-0s, Class B16, in 1919. As with the B7s, the final series of thirty-two engines appeared in 1923/4, making a class of seventy in all. In 1937 one was rebuilt with outside Walschaert valve gear and derived motion for the inside valve. Six more engines were rebuilt later to this standard, classified as B16/2. Thompson continued the rebuilding but with three independent sets of valve gear. There were fifteen LNER examples of this B16/3 variant, with two more added after nationalisation. On

B16 No. 1459 heading a No. 1 express goods at Potters Bar in September 1946, watched from the footpath by interested observers. D. A. DANT

While working a goods train bound for Whitemoor, B16 No. 1466 takes water at Spalding, in May 1947. L. R. PETERS

K3 No. 2425 at Digswell, the southern end of the two-track section from Woolmer Green, with an up express goods in 1934.
R. S. CARPENTER

the GNR, the K3 2-6-0s had been introduced in 1920 as a class of ten engines. They gained an early reputation for good performance by hauling very heavy passenger trains between between Doncaster and King's Cross during the 1921 coal strike. The design was multiplied by the LNER as a standard large mixed-traffic type. The Darlington drawing office adapted the GNR external features to meet the LNER composite loading gauge. The LNER-built engines were therefore visually quite different from the GNR examples which were not brought into line until the 1940s. The importance attached to express goods traffic by the LNER is illustrated by the building of batches of K3s during a time of general depression. After sixty had been built at Darlington in 1924/5, orders were placed in 1927/30 for forty-nine more which went into traffic in 1929/31. With the commencement of economic recovery, new K3s were again ordered in 1934 and when building ceased in 1937 the class totalled 193 engines.

Before the last K3s were built, the initial batch of Class V2 2-6-2s were at work. The V2s represented an entirely new concept of the mixed traffic locomotive. Like the P1s, the design owed much to contemporary Gresley Pacifics and provided a reserve of power not previously available for express goods work. Whereas the B7/B16/K3 mixed traffic generation had the capability of handling excursion and relief traffic at weekends, the V2s, with 6ft 2in diameter coupled wheels, were quite at home with most of the LNER express duties. They were of enormous value during the war and immediately afterwards when express trains were exceedingly heavy and many of the Pacifics were in a sadly run-down condition. By 1944, there were 184 V2s at work. In many respects the V2s were the ultimate LNER mixed traffic engines. A 6ft 2in Pacific had appeared in 1943 as a result of the rebuilding of a 2-8-2. The last four V2s on order were completed to a similar design but with a smaller firebox and cylinders. Eventually the A2 class of 6ft 2in Pacifics totalled forty engines of four distinct varieties, the final examples being built after nationalisation. In these engines the distinction between mixed traffic and express passenger types virtually disappeared.

Sources:
Minutes of LNER Locomotive Committee and LNER Joint Locomotive and Traffic Committee.

For this and succeeding chapters, much reference has been made to various parts of the RCTS Locomotives of the LNER series.

This view shows an up No. 1 express goods having just passed through York station headed by V2 No. 4777 on 21st August 1937.
H. C. DOYLE

Pressed into goods service, Thompson A2/1 No. 60509 Waverley *taking the down through road at Darlington on 16th June 1950.*
E. D. BRUTON

GNR 'Long Tom' 0–8–0 No. 417 with an up coal train passing the curious T-shaped Ganwick signal box. A. G. ELLIS

CHAPTER TWO

PETERBOROUGH TO LONDON COAL AND BRICK TRAFFIC

GNR 0–6–0 No. 377 heading north from Potters Bar with empty wagons. H. GORDON TIDEY

IN the earliest years of the Great Northern Railway the carriage of South Yorkshire coal provided an important portion of its receipts. With the addition of Nottinghamshire as a source, the traffic built up and remained a prominent feature of the GNR's and later the LNER's goods traffic operations. The early consignments from South Yorkshire to King's Cross goods station via the Lincolnshire loop line were the first large scale deliveries of coal to London by land transport.

The New England sidings north of Peterborough were established by the GNR as a major staging post in the long haul of coal south from the yards at Doncaster and Colwick where the wagons from the collieries were initially concentrated. Peterborough, situated almost exactly halfway between Doncaster and London, was no doubt a convenient point for engine changing and examination of trains; Wellingborough, dividing the Midland Railway's Toton to Brent route into two nearly equal portions was an exact counterpart. Nowadays block loads would be worked through without a break, but for the 0-6-0s of the nineteenth century, with their small fireboxes, the duration of the haul was quite sufficient. So quite apart from marshalling considerations, tradition was established and trains were staged at Peterborough throughout the history of the traffic.

At the London end the trains were originally worked to King's Cross goods station where a large coal yard was established. The growth of the railway network south of the Thames, linked to the GNR from 1866, gave rise to a large transfer traffic in coal. The marshalling requirements for this traffic resulted in the development of Ferme Park yard between Hornsey and Harringay, now replaced on the up side by a depot for electric suburban stock.

The development of brickworks, extending from Fletton to Yaxley on both sides of the main line south of Peterborough, added a considerable traffic in bricks for many years. This will be discussed with the coal traffic as the carriage of the two commodities was to some extent intermingled.

In early years successive generations of 0-6-0s provided the motive power. It is interesting to note that for fifty years, until the first Ivatt Long Tom 0-8-0 appeared in 1901, there was comparatively little increase in the size and power of the locomotives employed, the only exception being the short-lived steam tenders of Archibald Sturrock in 1865/6 With the advent of the 0-8-0s loads could be increased to 60 wagons in the loaded direction giving a weight of about 1,000 tons behind the tender. By the late 1920s the 'Long Toms' were rare visitors south of Peterborough, having been superseded by the Gresley O1 and O2 2-8-0s. The first O1 commenced work at the end of 1913 and from 1914 onwards eighty wagon loads of some 1,350 tons behind the tender were regularly worked. The two-cylinder O1s

The New England yards and Eastfield signal box, looking north from the Westwood bridge. MICHAEL BACK

were eventually joined by the three-cylinder O2s and these two classes bore the brunt of the traffic throughout the inter-war years. Some preference could be detected for the use of the O2s on the heavier through trains but by and large the two classes were interchangeable.

In 1925 the 2-8-0s were supplemented by the two P1 2-8-2s and later, in 1932, K3s were introduced on fast timings. The rather specialised utilisation of the last two classes is dealt with later when the services of 1935 are considered in detail.

During the 1939–1945 war the first Austerity WD 2-8-0s appeared and the consequent transfers of O1s and O2s brought to an end the dominance of the Gresley 2-8-0s. In the post-war period the Austerities became well established and, although they often looked unkempt and sounded rough, the reported opinions of the men who ran them were usually favourable. In 1955 they were joined at New England by the magnificent Class 9F 2-10-0s. The introduction of the 'Nines' was accompanied by some prohibitions on the use of station yards, authority as always reacting defensively to the use of engines with a long wheelbase. Before they finally gave way to diesels, however, it was not unusual to see a 9F, rubrics notwithstanding, on a pick-up goods happily shunting in yards laid out when a Stirling 0-6-0 was the largest engine to be found on such duties. Finally, the coal trains were handed over to Brush type 4 diesel-electrics (now class 47) for the short period of dwindling traffic between the official termination of steam haulage south of Peterborough in June 1963 and 1st August 1966 when the remaining through loads were transferred either to the Great Eastern line via Whitemoor or the Midland line to Brent.

The New England and Ferme Park yard at the ends of the route had more or less taken their final shape in the early 1900s. At New England (*Fig. 1*) all the sidings were on the up side of the main line, the down side being effectively closed in by the presence of the Midland line to

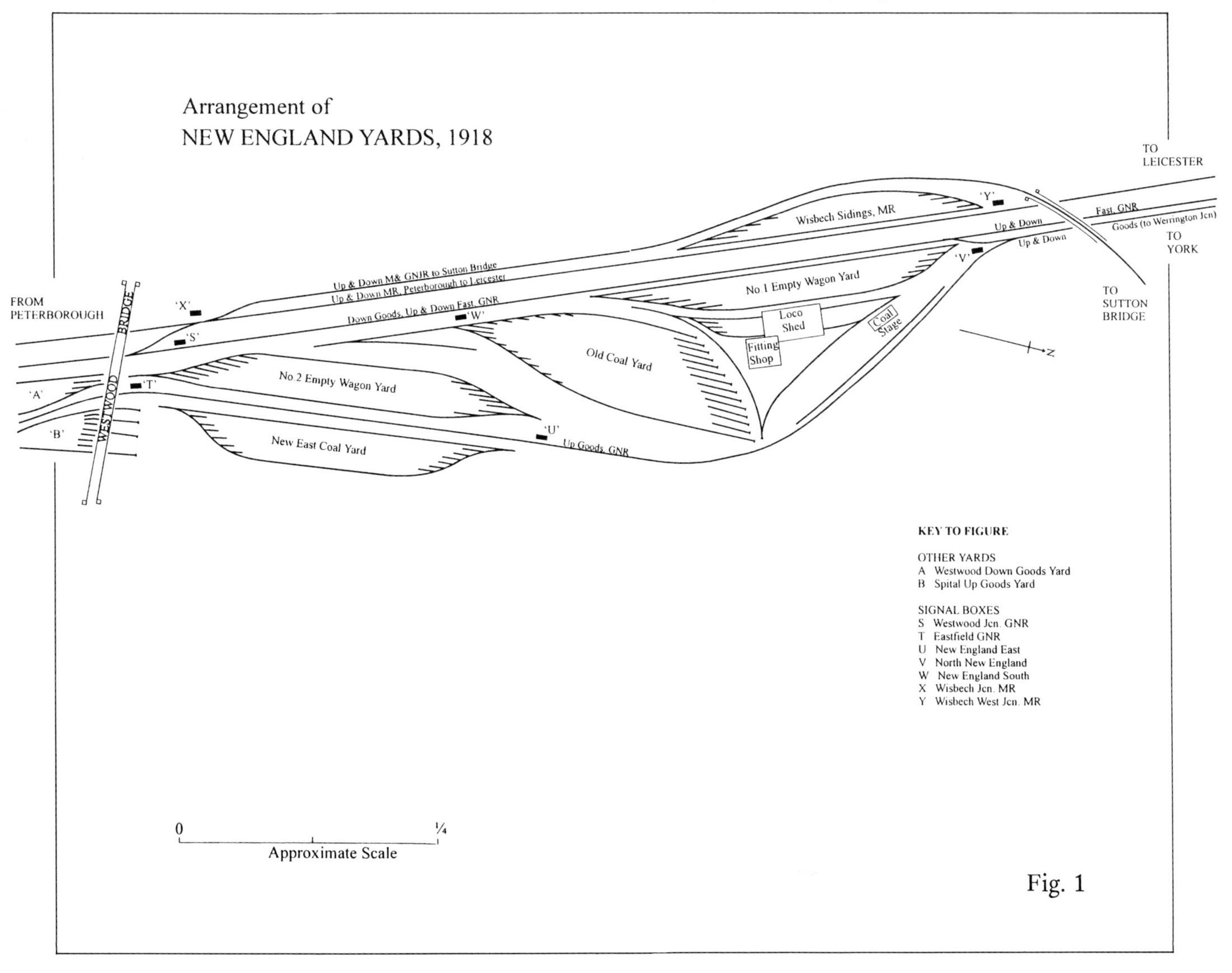

Fig. 1

Leicester. Empty wagons were sorted into particular colliery areas in No. 1 (old) and No. 2 (West) Empty Wagon Yards. No. 2 was a gravitation yard. Coal trains were broken up and re-marshalled in the Old Coal Yard which consisted of single-ended sidings and the New (gravitation) East Coal Yard. In the 1935 period, up trains were marshalled at New England into four sections classified as follows

Section No. 1. Southern Railway lines but excluding the LNER depots at Brockley and Elephant and Castle.
Section No. 2. High Barnet, Alexandra Palace and Edgware branches, Finsbury Park, Hackney Wick, Poplar, East India Dock and Lea Cut.
Section No. 3. King's Cross, Caledonian Road, Cambridge Street and other LNER depots:

Ashburton Grove	Harringay
Bow Common	Highbury Vale
Brockley	Hornsey
Clarence Yard	Hornsey Goods
Crews Hill	Hornsey Loco
Cuffley	LT & S Section
Elephant and Castle	

Section No. 4. Wood Green, Palmers Green, Winchmore Hill and Enfield.

The New England requirement in 1935 for pilot and shunting engines was:

No. 1. East Coal Yard	6.0 am Monday to 6.0 am Sunday
No. 2. Old Coal Yard	6.0 am Monday to 6.0 am Sunday
No. 3. West Empties Yard	6.0 am Monday to 2.0 pm Sunday
No. 4. Old Empties Yard	6.0 am to 10 pm daily, Sunday Excepted

Another five engines were required for the Spital and Westwood goods yards and the Peterborough North cripple yard.

New England provided standage for about 3,000 wagons total, loaded and empty, excluding capacity for about 1,000 wagons in the Spital and Westwood goods yards.

At Ferme Park (*Fig. 2*) the loaded and empty yards were on the up and down sides of the line respectively. Connection between the two sides was made by the Harringay flyover opened in 1893. Successive portions of the yards were opened in 1888, 1894 and 1899 in which last year the locomotive shed was completed. The building of the loco shed and the extension of the up sidings necessitated the diversion of the New River. Hornsey station was rebuilt in 1900 as a consequence of the works on the down side.

Wagons were marshalled at Ferme Park into trains for the various destinations noted above in the list of sections. The actual working of the transfer traffic is, however, a subject in itself. As with New England the total capacity of the Ferme Park yard was about 3,000 wagons and in 1935 four marshalling pilots were required:

No. 1. Up Side, Low Yard	6.0 am Monday to 6.0 am Sunday
No. 2. Up Side, Top Yard	6.0 am Monday to 6.0 am Sunday
No. 3. Down Side, South End	6.0 am Monday to 6.0 am Sunday

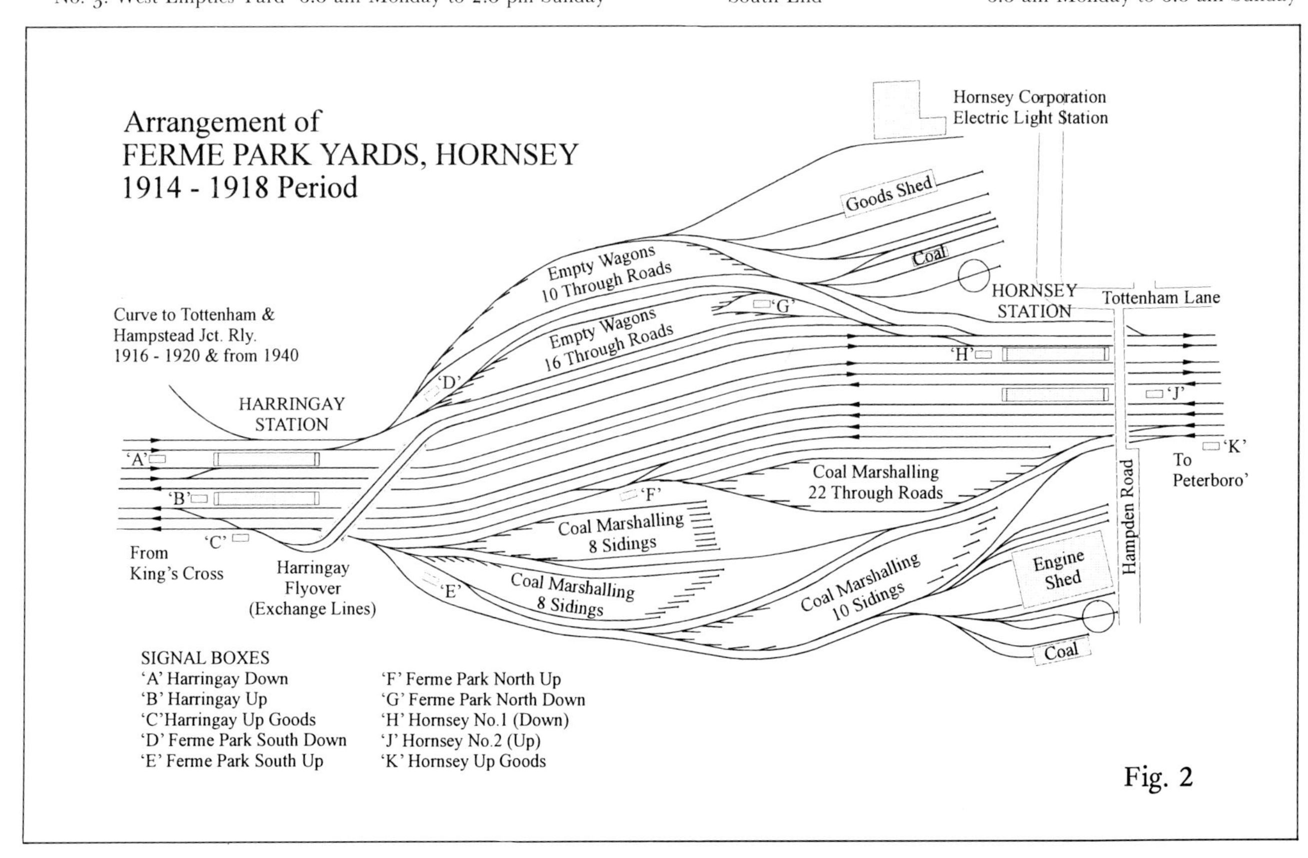

Fig. 2

No. 4. Down Side, Western Group	1.0 am Monday to 12.0 Midnight Sunday

Up trains were examined at New England. Although by 1935 grease-lubricated wagons were fast disappearing, examination in earlier years involved the wagon examiner tapping each wheel and then flipping open the top of the axle box with his hammer. If he saw sufficient grease he banged it shut again, otherwise he left it open for his lad who followed, struggling with the weight of his grease can, to fill the box. The oil-lubricated axlebox was a great step forward but the edict remained that down empties which left Ferme Park without examination had to be examined at Hitchin.

The ruling gradient of 1 in 200 meant that hard work was required with heavy loads. The longest stretch at that inclination was, however, against the empty trains, 8 miles from Wood Green to Potters Bar. On the up road the longest climb was the 8 miles from Arlesey to Stevenage with the last 5 miles at 1 in 200, a pitch which was always broken by a water stop at Hitchin. Another long 1 in 200 climb in the up direction was the 5 miles from Connington to beyond Abbots Ripton.

It was the time taken by loaded trains on the 1 in 200 banks that led to the first widening of the original double track line between Peterborough and King's Cross. As early as February 1853 Edmund Denison, in his

O2 No. 3482 with a down Class B goods train north of Hatfield in 1937. PHOTOMATIC

A down Class A empty wagon train, hauled by O4 No. 6635, being turned out onto the two-track section to Potters Bar at Greenwood box.
AUTHOR'S COLLECTION

O2 No. 3481 taking a Class A empty wagon train past an up coal train at Sandy on 25th May 1935. L. HANSON

A down No. 1 express goods passing Sandy on 25th May 1935 headed by K3 No. 91. L. HANSON

Chairman's address to the Half-yearly Ordinary General Meeting of the Great Northern Railway Co, had said:

> '... from London to Peterborough which is 76 miles, the line is so constructed that, with very little additional expense, two additional lines may be laid down; so that it would be a railway constructed to carry four lines. The embankments are already formed for four lines; the bridges are three arched bridges; so that an additional line would run through each of the side arches; ... I have asked Sir William Cubitt, and he says there will be no difficulty whatever, either with respect to tunnels or bridges, in laying down two additional lines; that the embankments are all wide enough for that and the land has been bought'

With the optimism typical of a Chairman addressing his shareholders he went on the predict that the four roads would be required in seven years time, i.e. by 1860. In actual fact the first widening anywhere north of Seven Sisters Road (later Finsbury Park) was the addition of an up loop from Hitchin to Wymondley in 1869. By 1874 this had been extended to Stevenage and a further loop had been completed from Hatfield to Potters Bar. Cubitt's statement on the ease of widening was to some extent vindicated by the low cost of some of these early works, the up goods from Hitchin through Wymondley to Stevenage costing no more than £3,258 per mile. But the Welwyn viaduct and the numerous tunnels south of the summit point at Woolmer Green were serious obstacles. Although sanction was obtained for widening from Potters Bar to Wood Green in the 1880s, no work was then carried out north of Greenwood, and another 70 years elapsed before the three new tunnels were bored between there and Potters Bar. In fact the piecemeal provision of additional lines had effectively ceased by the end of the nineteenth century, leaving odd sections as bottlenecks which caused serious delays and reduced the value of the quadrupled sections. So in 1935, as for many years previously, the two track sections were:

Yaxley to Connington
Leys turn-out to Huntington North No. 1 (Up main only but two down lines throughout)
Sandy Station
Arlesey Station
Woolmer Green to Digswell
Potters Bar to Greenwood

The additional lines were designated either 'slow' or 'goods' lines. The 'slow' lines were worked by Absolute Block and were used by both passenger and goods trains. The 'goods' lines were worked permissively and normally carried only goods traffic. The block instruments for the goods lines were divided into sectors labelled 'Line Clear', 'Line Blocked' and 'Line Occupied', the last named in place of the conventional 'Train on Line' designation. The regulation governing the admission of a train to an already occupied section stated:

> LINE OCCUPIED must always be given when the line between two signal boxes is not clear. When "line occupied" is received in

An unusually clean and probably newly ex-works J3 No. 4100 puffing out from the up goods line onto the two-track bottleneck through Sandy station on 1st May 1937. L. HANSON

K2 No. 4681 with a No. 2 express goods on the up fast line at Sandy on 1st May 1937. L. HANSON

The fireman of this J6 was relaxing as the engine passed through Sandy station with an up stopping goods c.1932. This lovely view also features A1 No. 4479 Robert the Devil *approaching with a down express.* G. H. SOOLE/NRM

reply to "is line clear", the signalman tendering "is line clear" must keep the signals which govern the line at danger until the train has been stopped at a home signal. He must then take off the home signal and show a caution signal by a green flag or hand lamp, held steadily in the hand, and, when such is practicable, verbally instruct the engineman to proceed cautiously.

The difficulties caused by the bottlenecks were minimised where possible by designating the last section of additional line on the approach side as 'goods' and providing a turnout at the previous block post from the slow to fast lane. Hence two or more goods trains could be held on the goods line while they were overtaken by a slow passenger train turned out behind them on to the fast line. Typical examples of this layout were the sections of up goods from Everton to Sandy and from Knebworth to Woolmer Green and the down goods from New Barnet North to Greenwood.

The characteristics of the line made particular demands on the engineman. At Sandy, for instance, the brake van of a short train standing at the up goods home signal could not be sighted from a following train at a long distance due to three overbridges situated on a left-hand curve. This demanded particular care by drivers of trains approaching from Everton. At Potters Bar, after spending possibly as long as half an hour waiting for the road, the driver of an up goods was often hustled down to Greenwood by the signalman shouting through his megaphone 'Express passed Hitchin'. Controlling a train totalling some 1,450 tons with engine, tender and guard's brakes only through the short block sections, and getting it turned in smartly on the slow line at Greenwood, must have been no easy task. The running time for Class B, C and D trains through the unwidened section was 8 minutes, to which was added 3 minutes for starting and 2 minutes for turning in, 13 minutes in all.

During the 1914–1918 war the tonnage of coal conveyed south from Peterborough rose to an unprece-

TABLE 2
COAL & BRICK TRAINS, NEW ENGLAND TO FERME PARK
Tuesdays to Fridays, Autumn 1935

Train No.		69	108	307	312	328	345	355	406	463	697	739	810	837
Load		Bricks	Coal	Bricks	Coal	Coal	Coal	Coal	Coal	Coal	Bricks	Coal	Bricks	Bricks
Class		C	A	C	A	C	C	C	C	C	C	C	C Q	C
		a.m.	a.m.	a.m.	a.m.	a.m.	a.m.	a.m.	p.m.	p.m.	p.m.	p.m.	p.m.	p.m.
NEW ENGLAND	dep	*3.20K*	6.30	*7.0K*	8.25	9.15	9.50	10.15	12.25	1.25	*4.55K*	6.55	*7.25K*	9.5
FLETTON	arr	*3.35K*	-	*7.15K*	-	-	-	-	-	-	*5.10K*	-	*7.40K*	-
	dep	4.5	-	7.45	-	-	-	-	-	-	5.25	-	8.20	-
Yaxley	arr	4.15	-	-	-	-	-	-	-	-	-	-	-	9.25
	dep	5.0	-	8.48	-	-	10.22	11.6	1.2	-	6.5	7.44	9.15	10.23
Holme	dep	-	-	-	-	-	-	-		-	-	8.17	-	-
Leys	dep	6.30	pass	9.42	pass	10.30	11.20	11.58	1.59	-	-	9.22	10.25	11.26
Huntingdon	dep	-	7.22	-	9.17	-	-	-	-	-	-	-	-	-
Offord (Water Stop)	arr	6.52	-	10.6	-	10.52	11.44	12.21	2.23	2.59	7.12	9.46	10.47	11.50
	dep	6.57	-	10.11	-	10.57	11.49	12.26	2.28	3.4	7.17	9.51	10.52	11.57
St. Neots	dep	-	pass	-	pass	-	pass	-	-	3.50	-	-	-	-
Sandy	dep	7.55	7.50	-	9.53	-	12.33	-	-	-	9.9	-	-	-
Arlesley	dep	-	-	-	-	12.12	-	-	3.45	-	-	-	-	-
Hitchin (Water Stop)	arr	8.45	8.22	11.50	10.23	12.40	1.44	2.17	4.8	5.23	10.1	11.25	12.28	1.27
	dep	9.15	8.40	12.5	10.33	12.50	1.54	2.27	4.17	5.33	10.19	11.35	12.38	1.37
Knebworth	dep	-	-	-	11.8	-	-	-	-	-		-		
Woolmer Green	dep	-	-	-	-	2.18	-	-	5.0	6.52		-		
Hatfield	arr	-	pass	12.58	pass	pass	-	pass	pass	pass	H	pass	H	H
	dep	10.29	9.20	1.36	11.26	2.35	2.50	3.20	5.19	7.11		12.40		
Potters Bar	dep	11.22	9.48	2.38	-	-	4.8	4.31	5.48	-		1.2		
Wood Green	dep	-	-	-	-	-	-	-	-	-	12.12	-	2.34	4.5
FERME PARK	arr	12.10	10.18	3.25	12.0	3.35	5.0	5.10	7.30	8.22	12.20	1.50	2.45	4.13

NOTES
- H via Hertford Loop
- K Engine & Brake Van
- Q Runs when required
- 0.0 Stands for other trains to pass

TABLE 3
CLASS 'A' EMPTY TRAINS, FERME PARK TO NEW ENGLAND
Tuesdays to Fridays, Autumn 1935

Train No.		16	50	116	160	341	433	514	574a	715 Q	730	738a	819	828
		a.m.	a.m.	a.m.	a.m.	a.m.	p.m.	p.m.	p.m.	p.m.	p.m.	p.m.	p.m.	p.m.
FERME PARK	dep	12.40	1.40	5.10	6.10	11.15	1.5	2.0	3.55	7.0	7.55	8.25	10.40	11.50
Wood Green	dep	12.50	-	-	-	pass	pass	pass	4.4	-	-	8.40	10.50	-
Greenwood	dep		-	-	-	11.40	1.27	2.54		8.10	8.49			12.25
Hatfield	arr	H	pass	pass	pass	12.12	1.56	pass	H	pass	pass	H	H	pass
	dep		2.48	6.4	6.58	12.16	1.59	3.18		8.36	9.12			12.47
Digswell	dep		-	-	-	-	2.12	3.37		-	-			-
Hitchin (Water Stop)	arr	2.22	3.31	6.44	7.55	pass	pass	4.11	6.23	9.25	9.55	10.18	12.28	1.25
	dep	2.32	3.41	6.54	8.0	12.48	2.37	4.21	6.43	9.35	10.5	10.27	12.38	1.37
Biggleswade	arr	-	4.15	-	-	-	-	-	-	-	-	-	-	A
	dep	-	4.45	-	-	-	-	-	-	-	-	-	-	-
Sandy	arr	-	-	pass	-	pass	pass	-	-	-	-	11.6	-	-
	dep	-	-	7.30	-	1.9	2.58	5.16	-	-	10.50	11.22	1.18	-
St. Neots	dep	-	-	-	-	-	-	-	-	-	-	-	-	-
Offord (Water Stop)	arr	-	5.21	8.4	9.0	-	-	5.48	7.50	10.34	11.19	11.51	1.47	2.43
	dep	-	5.26	8.9	9.5	-	-	5.53	7.55	10.39	11.24	11.56	1.52	2.48
Huntingdon	arr	3.34	pass	pass	pass	pass	pass	pass	pass	pass	pass	pass	pass	pass
	dep	3.59	5.36	8.19	9.15	1.35	3.24	6.3	8.5	10.49	11.34	12.6	2.2	2.58
Conington	dep	-	6.8	9.3	-	-	-	8.5	9.49	12.18	1.59	2.27	2.40	-
Yaxley	arr	4.40	-	-	-	-	-	-	-	-	-	-	-	-
	dep	4.50	-	-	-	-	-	-	-	-	-	-	-	-
FLETTON	arr	5.0	-	9.27	-	-	-	-	-	-	2.23	-	-	-
	dep	5.12	-		-	-	-	-	-	-		-	-	3.36
Crescent Jcn.	dep	-	6.53		-	-	-	-	-	-		-	-	4.12
NEW ENGLAND	arr	5.32	7.1		10.45	2.20	4.5	8.45	10.20	12.58		3.5	3.49	4.22

NOTES
- A Arlesley 1.57 a.m.
- H via Hertford Loop
- Q Runs when required
- 0.0 Stands for other trains to pass

The solitary W1 No. 10000 taking its turn in freight service to head an up goods at Potters Bar on 30th March 1946. D. A. DANT

dented peak. This was due to the suspension of all carriage of coal by sea from the North East Coast ports to Southern England. By 1917, aided by the Great Northern's recently completed traffic control system, some 40 trains or about 2,000 wagons per week were being worked direct from Colwick to Ferme Park with Colwick men throughout, in addition to about 100 trains or 5,000 wagons per week from New England. The through Colwick to Ferme Park trains did not survive the return to normal conditions and, with the resumption of coastal shipping and the general depression of trade, the coal traffic of 1935 was greatly reduced. This was to some extent offset by the growth of the Fletton brick traffic, a large demand for bricks having been created by speculative building in the London suburbs.

In order to reduce wartime congestion in the suburban area, the final northern section from Cuffley to Langley of the Hertford loop was temporarily completed as a single line and opened for goods traffic on 4th March 1918. Traffic was worked over the entire 14¾ miles of the newly opened portion as a single section. In order to obtain a reasonable traffic capacity over such a long single line section, Tyers No. 5 Absolute and Permissive Tablet System was installed. This was the first application in Great Britain of a permissive signalling system on a single line. When the section was already occupied, the driver of a train entering would in addition to the usual warning, be handed the 'permissive' tablet in a special pouch as a further reminder. A 'tidal flow' timetable was instituted under which up trains had the use of the line for part of the day and down trains for the remainder. The system was used until the line was doubled at the end of 1920.

One aspect of the system for which no explanation is now available is the method by which trains were safely despatched through the Ponsbourne tunnel, close to the Cuffley end of the section, which at 2,684 yds was the longest on the GNR. Although there is no doubt that the section for permissive working extended from Cuffley to Langley, it is almost certain that some form of auxiliary control was adopted to ensure that two trains did not occupy the tunnel simultaneously. The other tunnel in the section, Molewood, is short and would not have provided any sighting problems.

In the up direction the Hertford loop was no harder than the main line, the ruling gradient of 1 in 198 being practically identical with the 1 in 200 of the latter. On the down road, however, the climb over the Wood Green flyover at 1 in 57 was a serious disadvantage. Paradoxically, more use was made of the down road than the up, probably because of the ease of arranging departures from Ferme Park to phase in with the passenger traffic and the uncertainty of the times of the up trains by the time Hertford North was reached.

The absence of any running loops or refuge sidings was a serious limitation of the capacity for a combination of mineral and suburban traffic south of Hertford. Although the platforms at Gordon Hill, like those of the roughly contemporary Letchworth, were shaped to allow the provision of passenger loops, these were never laid in, the only use of the outer faces being an up bay for suburban trains.

Unless specially ordered by Control, no coal or goods trains were allowed to leave Langley via the loop between 3.30 am and 8.0 pm except for the daily pick-up goods.

Table 2 shows details of the timings in Autumn 1935 of those Class A and C coal and brick trains which carried a substantially through load to Ferme Park. There were other trains which stopped en route to set down portions but for simplicity these have had to be omitted. Also for simplicity the many variations on Mondays and Saturdays have been ignored but the table is valid for

O2 No. 3490 at Greenwood in 1936 with an up coal train which, as can be seen, also included two bogie brick wagons as the leading vehicles. C. R. L. COLES

Tuesdays to Fridays. *Table 3* shows the timings of the empty wagon trains (all of which were Class A) equivalent to the up trains of *Table 2*. The working timetable also laid down point to point running times for extras and trains running out of course. Allowing for water stops, these between New England and Ferme Park amounted approximately to:

Up	Class A	195 minutes
Up	Class C	310 minutes
Down	Class A	200 minutes

When compared with the actual bookings, the large amount of time lost in waiting for paths at bottlenecks becomes obvious.

The first train in *Table 2*, No. 69 up brick, got perhaps the worst road of all. The engine and brake left New England at 3.20 am to pick up the load at Fletton and Yaxley. Leaving Yaxley at 5.0 am, there were waits of some 45 minutes at Leys, 18 at Sandy, 23 at Hatfield, and finally 28 minutes at Potters Bar. In addition, the Hitchin water stop was extended by 20 minutes. In all, therefore, including the making up of the train at Fletton and Yaxley, the engine was out on the road for 8 hours and 50 minutes. As with the other Class C trains, a 5 minute stop was booked at Offord for water in addition to the Hitchin stop (made actually at Cambridge Junction). The Working Time Table stated that Class C trains must stop at Hitchin for water and will only stop at Offord (and at Biggleswade) for water when necessary. From memory of limited observations, the Offord stop was usually made in the up direction and usually omitted going down. With nose to the stable there was an incentive to press on with an empty wagon train, but with the heavier loaded trains the stop gave 5 minutes respite and relaxation. A summer evening at Offord is remembered with an O2 quietly simmering while the tank was filling, the men snatching a sit down on the platform seat, then boarding, touching the whistle for the gates and home board, then snaking away round the banks of the Ouse, an idyllic scene in surroundings far removed from the world of collieries and marshalling yards.

No. 108, the 6.30 am from New England, was the first of two daily Class A coal trains. Introduced in 1932, these fast workings reduced congestion and at the same time enabled a crew to make the journey from New England to Ferme Park and back in one shift. Extra time was allowed for No. 108 at Cambridge Junction so that the 7.34 am passenger from Cambridge, leaving Hitchin at 8.39 am, could be followed. Otherwise a clear road was booked. The second Class A train was No. 312, the 8.25 am from New England, which was booked to Ferme Park in 3 hours 35 minutes. K3 locomotives were used for these workings with a load of 56 wagons of coal and, to ensure sufficient brake power was available, a loaded vacuum-fitted 50 ton bogie brick wagon was marshalled next to the engine and a 20 ton brake van was provided. For train loading purposes, a loaded 'bogie brick' was reckoned as equal to four loaded 10-ton wagons. An empty bogie brick was equivalent to three empty 10 ton wagons. In the down direction the load was 60 empty wagons and a 20 ton brake van. At Ferme Park the New England crews were

An up Class C coal train drawn by O1 No. 3462 at Stratford Brook, south of Sandy, in 1928. L&GRP

K2 No. 4659 with a down Class A train of empty wagons at Sandy on 1st May 1937. L. HANSON

P1 No. 2394 at Langley troughs with an up coal train.

H. GORDON TIDEY

P1 No. 2394 taking an up coal train through Potters Bar station.
AUTHOR'S COLLECTION

relieved by Hornsey men who turned, watered and possibly coaled the engine, then took it over the flyover and put it on the train for the return trip. The engine and men of No. 108 up returned with the No. 341 down (*Table 3*), the equivalent working for No. 312 up being No. 433 down. Turn round times of 57 and 65 minutes were thus booked and that these quick turn rounds were actually achieved in practice is shown by the following observations made at Wood Green:

Date	*Engine No.*	*Train*	*Pass Wood Green*	*Train*	*Pass Wood Green*
18.6.35	120	108U	11.0 am	341D	12.06 pm
25.6.35	126	108U	11.12 am	341D	12.30 pm
1.7.35	206	108U	10.14 am	341D	11.32 pm
8.7.35	2672	108U	11.0 am	341D	12.12 pm
18.6.35	4007	312U	12.49 pm	433D	2.0 pm
25.6.35	125	312U	12.47 pm	433D	2.6 pm
1.7.35	4003	312U	11.56 am	433D	1.8 pm
8.7.35	204	312U	12.29 pm	433D	1.36 pm

Successful operation of such trains demanded fairly close adherence to booked times; the slower trains, however, had no claim to priority and often were to be found well outside their booked paths.

No. 307 was an up brick train with somewhat similar timings to No. 69. The engine left New England Loco at 6.45 am, and the Hatfield stop was presumably made to put off part of the load.

No. 328 up, the first of a series of Class C coal trains, was booked for a P1 and loaded to 100 wagons The WTT note stated:

> Working of 100 wagon trains by Mikado Engines between New England and London.
>
> Following train is worked by Mikado engine and conveys 100 wagons between New England and London.
>
> 328 (9.15 am New England to Ferme Park), Mondays and Saturdays inclusive.
>
> Approximate length of train is 670 yards and must be worked with 20 ton brake.
>
> In the event of the Up Home signals at Connington being at danger, drivers must draw well up to them before bringing the trains to a stand, so as to clear safety catch 701 yards north of Up Home signals.
>
> Trains must run on Up Goods line Connington to Abbots Ripton or Leys; Huntington North No. 1 to Offord or beyond; and Arlesey to Cambridge Junction. They must also run on Up Slow or Good lines, Hitchin to Knebworth or Woolmer Green. Engines to take water Cambridge Junction.

Four Class C coals trains followed, Nos. 345, 355, 406 and 463 up. Their overall times were remarkably similar, ranging only from 6 hours 55 minutes to 7 hours 10 minutes. The only specific WTT note was for No. 355 defining the load as 80 wagons with a 20 ton brake van.

The first of three evening departures of brick trains was that of No. 697 up from Yaxley at 6.5 pm. During its wait of over an hour for the road through Sandy station, it was booked to be passed by three express trains, the evening Parly, a No. 1 Braked Goods (fish, Hull to King's Cross) and a No. 2 Braked Goods, the 2.40 pm from York Dringhouses, to King's Cross. There was ample time to clean and de-clinker the fire during such waits. The departure from Hitchin was not until 10.19 pm so the Hertford loop was available and, with no hindrance to the running, the fastest Class C Hitchin to Ferme Park time of the day, 2 hours 1 minute, was scheduled.

No. 739 up, the last Class C coal train of the day from New England, was notable in being booked to shunt at

A vacuum-fitted bogie brick wagon, providing additional braking power for K3 No. 61862, seen emerging from Hadley Wood South tunnel to be turned into the up slow line at Greenwood box on 23rd April 1949.

E. D. BRUTON

An up coal train with some brick wagons leading at Brookmans Park in the charge of K3 No. 1869 on 31st August 1947.
E. D. BRUTON

Holme in order to be passed by the 5.30 pm express from Leeds and the same Dringhouses to King's Cross goods that passed No. 697 at Sandy.

Table 2 is completed by two brick trains both using the Hertford loop and conforming to a general pattern of departures of coal in the day and bricks in the evening and early morning. The conditional No. 810 up ran through in times comparable with No. 697 but without the long wait at Sandy. No. 837 stopped at Hertford North from 2.35 am to 3.5 am in order to detach brick traffic for Chadwell Heath which was then worked across to Hertford East and so on to the Great Eastern Section. By the time No. 837 arrived at Ferme Park another day's traffic was starting with No. 69 moving up from Fletton to Yaxley to pick up the remainder of its load.

Although the empty loads permitted all the workings shown in *Table 3* to be Class A there were some variations in the timings. The return workings, Nos. 341 and 343 down, associated with the up Class A coals trains were significantly faster than the remainder. The first train in *Table 3*, No. 16 down, actually commenced its journey a King's Cross goods, leaving there at 12.5 am with wagons for Huntington North, St. Ives and similar destinations detached at Huntingdon North and also wagons for Biggleswade, Sandy and St. Neots which were detached at Ferme Park to go forward on No. 58 down (not listed) which left at 2.10 am. After picking up what was probably the major portion of its load at Ferme Park, No. 16 left at 12.40 am and travelled via the Hertford loop. Stops were made at Yaxley and Fletton to detach brick empties when necessary. The water stop shown for No. 50 down was made at Hitchin South. It then stopped again at Hitchin station in order to pick up mails unloaded from No. 23 down, 12.27 am No. 2 Braked Goods King's Cross goods to Grimsby. The mails were set down at Biggleswade. A call had earlier been made at New Southgate to attach, the full load being 80 wagons with a 10 ton brake van. No. 116 down took a similar load, in this case brick empties for Fletton.

No. 160 down was booked for an unusually clear road and made New England in 4 hours 35 minutes. Nos. 341 and 433 down have already been discussed with the up Class A trains. No. 514 down stopped at New Barnet from 2.25 pm to 2.45 pm to attach and make up the standard empty load of 80 wagons with a 10-ton brake van. No. 574a travelled via the Hertford loop. It was also made up to 80 wagons, stopping at Enfield Chase to attach from 4.22 pm to 4.44 pm. The traverse of the loop in the midst of suburban traffic was made by passing Wood Green 5 minutes after the departure of a Hertford North passenger, then at Enfield Chase it was passed by a second Hertford North train. The next down passenger terminated at Gordon Hill so No. 574a could clear Hertford North at 5.24 pm, 14 minutes before the next arrival.

The next four trains call for little comment. No. 715 down was a conditional working. No. 730 down terminated at Fletton and Nos. 738a and 819 down both ran via the Hertford loop. Nos. 730 and 738a had exceptional waits of about 1¾ hours each at Connington.

No. 828 down conveyed a full load for Colwick which was then worked forward intact from New England, presumably forming the next through departure, No. 99 down at 6.45 am arriving at Colwick at 9.1 am.

Many aspects of transport history reflect similarities on a larger scale of social history. The leisurely carriage of coal that has been described, mostly in private owners wagons eventually to be unloaded in a multitude of small coal yards, was possibly an indication of a less stereotyped and more relaxed way of life than our present age. The grid transmission lines and the gas distribution pipelines that supplanted the widespread distribution of coal have undoubtedly brought many benefits in their wake but let the last word rest with the late Eric Neve who, in providing invaluable information and advice for this chapter, wrote "What wouldn't I give to see a coal train slogging up the line nowadays."

Source: Great Northern Section Main Line Working Time Table, 1935.

Fig. 3

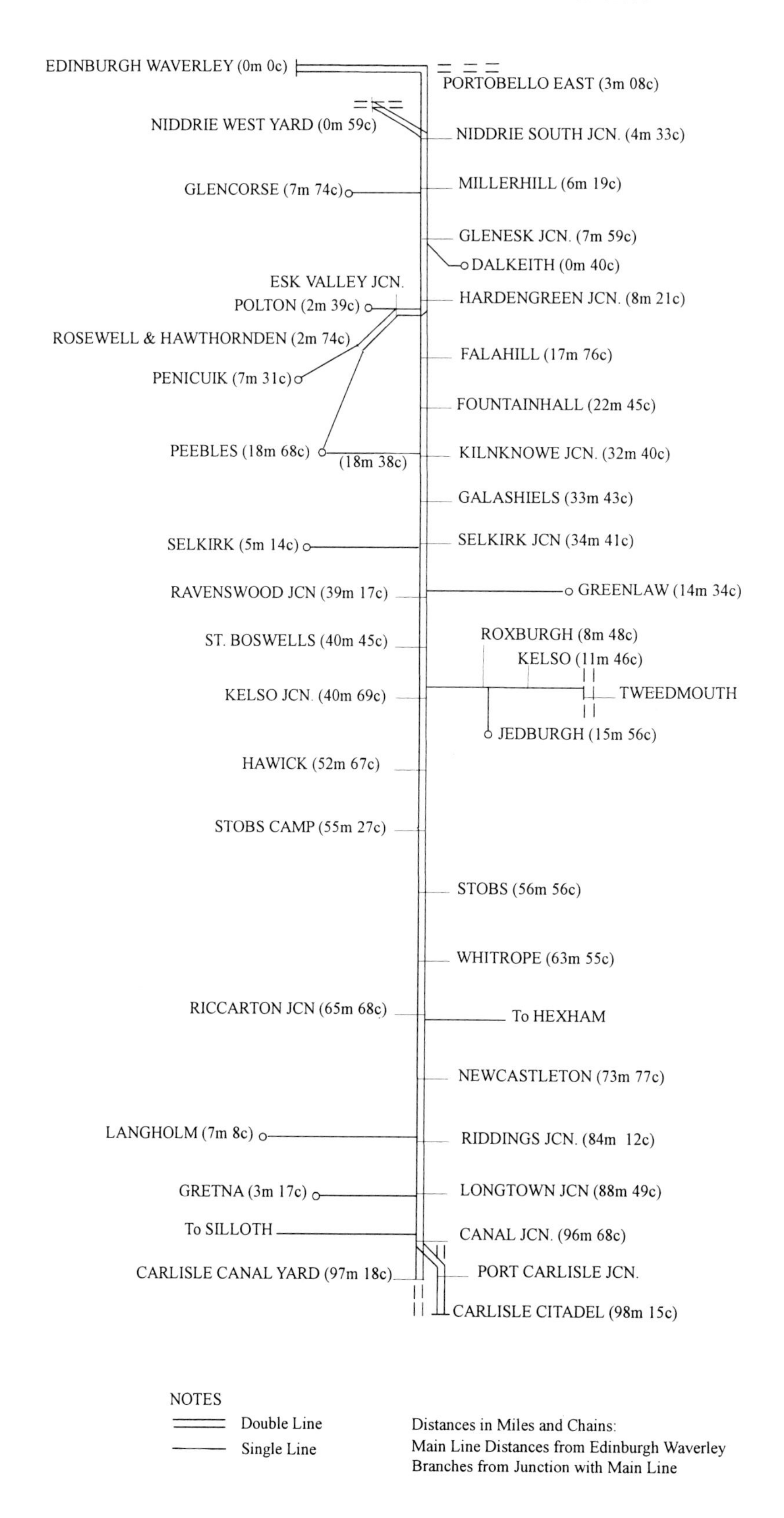
THE WAVERLEY ROUTE with Branches
EDINBURGH WAVERLEY (0m 0c)
PORTOBELLO EAST (3m 08c)
NIDDRIE WEST YARD (0m 59c)
NIDDRIE SOUTH JCN. (4m 33c)
GLENCORSE (7m 74c)
MILLERHILL (6m 19c)
GLENESK JCN. (7m 59c)
DALKEITH (0m 40c)
ESK VALLEY JCN.
POLTON (2m 39c)
HARDENGREEN JCN. (8m 21c)
ROSEWELL & HAWTHORNDEN (2m 74c)
FALAHILL (17m 76c)
PENICUIK (7m 31c)
FOUNTAINHALL (22m 45c)
PEEBLES (18m 68c)
(18m 38c)
KILNKNOWE JCN. (32m 40c)
GALASHIELS (33m 43c)
SELKIRK (5m 14c)
SELKIRK JCN (34m 41c)
RAVENSWOOD JCN (39m 17c)
GREENLAW (14m 34c)
ST. BOSWELLS (40m 45c)
ROXBURGH (8m 48c)
KELSO (11m 46c)
KELSO JCN. (40m 69c)
TWEEDMOUTH
JEDBURGH (15m 56c)
HAWICK (52m 67c)
STOBS CAMP (55m 27c)
STOBS (56m 56c)
WHITROPE (63m 55c)
RICCARTON JCN (65m 68c)
To HEXHAM
NEWCASTLETON (73m 77c)
LANGHOLM (7m 8c)
RIDDINGS JCN. (84m 12c)
GRETNA (3m 17c)
LONGTOWN JCN (88m 49c)
To SILLOTH
CANAL JCN. (96m 68c)
CARLISLE CANAL YARD (97m 18c)
PORT CARLISLE JCN.
CARLISLE CITADEL (98m 15c)
NOTES
Double Line
Single Line
Distances in Miles and Chains:
Main Line Distances from Edinburgh Waverley
Branches from Junction with Main Line

CHAPTER THREE

THE WAVERLEY ROUTE AND ITS BRANCHES

A J36 banking an up goods out of Hawick at the foot of the climb to Whitrope box. P. SUNDERLAND

TO some extent the contents of this chapter contradict the general title. The period considered in detail is the summer of 1951, more than three years after the LNER ceased to exist. This, however, only serves to emphasise a characteristic feature of the Waverley route, namely the long persistence of traffic patterns shaped by competition in earlier eras. Links with the past were underlined by the retention in the Working Time Table of references to most of the pre-grouping companies by their initials some 28 years after their demise. Of greater antiquity was the term Lanky by which the ex-LNWR line was still known at Carlisle. This recalled not the Lancashire and Yorkshire which was thus abbreviated further south but the LNW's local ancestor, the Lancaster and Carlisle Railway. For the train working arrangements detailed in this chapter the actual abbreviations and descriptions used in the 1951 WTT have been repeated.

The entry to Carlisle, so long desired by the North British, was accomplished in 1862 when the Border Union Railway was opened as an extension of the 1849 Hawick branch. The complete Edinburgh to Carlisle line was then advertised by the NBR as the Waverley route. Fourteen years were to elapse before full justification for its contstruction was achieved in 1876 with the completion of the Midland's Settle and Carlisle line. But even with the through Midland traffic, the Waverley route throughout its life must have been a doubtful asset due to its operating difficulties. A diagram of the line together with its branches as existing in 1951 is shown in *Fig. 3*.

The 98 miles from Edinburgh to Carlisle, mostly through superb scenery, were beset by incessant curvature and fearsome gradients. The latter included, northbound, 10 miles from beyond Newcastleton to Whitrope box nearly all at 1 in 75, and 16 miles from Galashiels to Falahill box averaging about 1 in 150. The cumulative total of all the adverse gradients from Carlisle to Edinburgh was equivalent to a vertical rise of no less than 1,930 feet.

The worst bank was encountered coming south, the 10½ miles from Hardengreen Junction to Falahill being nearly all at 1 in 70. On the Border Union Section, the

J67 0–6–0Ts Nos. 68511 and 68492 at Galashiels on 10th July 1950. To meet the weight restrictions of the Lauder Light Railway, they worked with empty side tanks. Ex-NBR tenders were attached to provide a water supply. A. G. ELLIS

11 miles from Hawick to Whitrope included some 7 miles at 1 in 80 or steeper. The Peebles and Penicuik branches shared a 1 in 53 bank for nearly 3 miles from Hardengreen Junction to Rosewell & Hawthornden. Banking assistance was regularly provided for goods trains going up to Falahill southbound and to Whitrope from both Hawick and Newcastleton. Banking was also authorised in the down direction from Galashiels to Falahill, and on the Peebles branch to Leadburn from Hardengreen Junction and Peebles Engine Shed box in up and down directions respectively. Apart from sections where assistance was available, trains faced ruling gradients of 1 in 100 going north and 1 in 120 in the opposite direction. The route traversed some exposed moorland, and snow could be a problem in winter. The provision of loops and refuge sidings was sparse but the long intervals between passenger trains enabled goods traffic to have a generally clear run. Express passenger working was hampered by the downhill restraint imposed by the curvature; the overall timings of expresses and the faster of the fitted goods trains differed by comparatively small amounts.

The operating difficulties in the main line were offset by a virtual absence of restrictions on locomotive availability. Edinburgh to Carlisle was passed both in LNER days and subsequently for Group 9 engines, i.e. all LNER classes. The sole limitation was that Pacifics, V2s and the W1 could be piloted only by 4-4-0s. The branches in general were passed for Group 6 engines with the addition of classes J37 and J38 and, in the case of the loop from Hardengreen through Peebles to Galashiels, also class K3. This meant that in practice there was no restriction on likely goods motive power. An exception to the general rule for the branches was the St. Boswells, Kelso and Tweedmouth line, over which locomotives of Groups 8 and 9 were permitted only in emergency at restricted speed. The provision was especially valuable for the diversions following the 1948 flood damage to the East Coast line. A second exception was the Lauder Light Railway which had a maximum permitted axle load of 12 tons. Latterly the problem of providing adequate power on this branch was solved by using GER J67 0-6-0Ts with empty tanks and a separate tender for the water supply.

The various generations of North British goods engines all played their part on the Waverley route. By the time of grouping, examples still remained of the classes which became LNER J31 to J34 inclusive; Hawick, in particular, possessed six J31s and six J33s. But their numbers were small compared with the three NB standard classes, nicely graded in size, designated by the LNER as J36, J35 and J37. The reason for the odd order of the classification remains a mystery. When superheated by the LNER, the J35s had a boiler standard with the J37s, although the latter, with larger valves and cylinders, were more powerful. It was the smallest of the NB standards, the J36s, however, that had the longest association with the route. Their use on banking, transfer trips and general light goods duties lasted well into the 1960s, some 75 or more years after their introduction.

In its last decade the North British shared certain characteristics with the Midland. Both were pioneers of train control systems and as a result both produced a grading of motive power according to haulage capability.

With the sole exception of the NB Atlantics, magnificently different, both lines relied to the end on a standardised family of 4-4-0s for passenger work and 0-6-0s for goods. The North British was, however, considering the merits of larger goods engines and held trials on Glenfarg Bank in 1921 with a GWR 2-8-0 and an NER 0-8-0, although the imminence of grouping precluded any actual new construction. It is not surprising, therefore, that the impact of the LNER on Waverley route motive power was in the introduction of larger locomotives for the through workings. The K3s, in particular, made their mark and the celebrated stud of A3s at Canal also took their turn on goods workings. But in the later years of steam haulage, if the use of any type on the route could be termed typical, then it would be V2s which must be nominated for the honour.

From the operating point of view the signalling of the line was conventional, although boasting a fine variety of signal box architecture. Some 28 block posts were open day and night during the week. The longest block section

J36 No. 9358 at Portobello on 6th August 1935. L. HANSON

J35 No. 9129 at Portobello on 6th August 1935. L. HANSON

J35 No. 64517 taking the branch line at Monktonhall Junction with empty wagons for local collieries on 28th June 1954.

E. D. BRUTON

was just over 7 miles from Riddings Junction to Kershopefoot, Penton Box only being opened when required for shunting. At Galashiels an early centralised signalling scheme was brought into use in 1937; a new box replaced the old North, Central and South boxes together with Kilnknowe and Selkirk junctions. At the northern end of the route an interesting development was completed in 1915 as a result of the large increase in tonnage of coal transported by rail from the Lothian coalfield. The scale of the increase was from 1,739,107 tons in 1903 to 3,653,938 tons in 1913. The resulting congestion and delays on the line south and east of Portobello led to the North British spending £220,000 on the construction of the Lothian lines shown in *Fig. 4*. These paralleled existing routes but provided alternative paths avoiding the flat junctions that had been the cause of delays. The Lothian lines included one of the first applications of an extension to the Sykes lock and block system to permit non-token working on single lines. The three single lines from Niddrie West Junction, Niddrie South Junction and Wanton Walls Junction all converged at Brunstane Park Junction and continued as a single line to South Leith Junction.

The previous connection from the East Coast main line at Niddrie East Junction was transferred to Monktonhall Junction so that traffic from the Smeaton line could

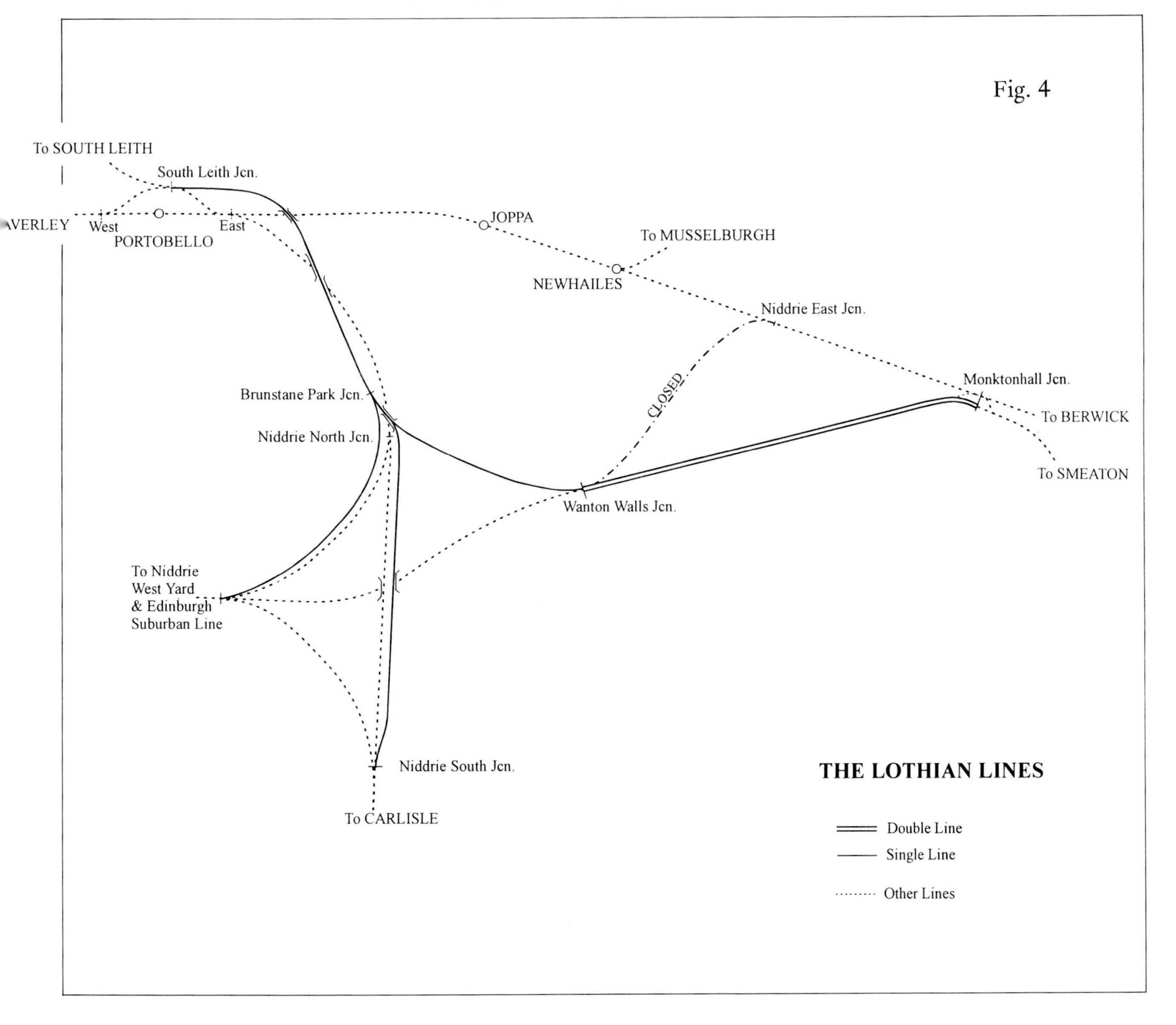

Heaton V2 No. 60952 with the 3.24 p.m. Millerhill to Heaton Class E joining the East Coast main line at Monktonhall Junction on 28th June 1951. E. D. BRUTON

A3 No. 60087 Blenheim *on the 2.42 p.m. Class E goods from Carlisle Canal to Niddrie South Yard approaching Shankend on 30th May 1961.*
J. F. AYLARD

proceed towards Wanton Walls without conflicting with movements on the main line. In 1926 the Waverley route box at Niddrie North Junction was closed and control of its points and signals transferred to a second frame which was added to the Brunstane Park Junction box. This latter box was then renamed Niddrie North Junction.

The congestion that gave rise to the Lothian lines was also the spur for the establishment of the NBR's first train control office at Portobello in August 1913. This was the first attempt in Scotland at central control of traffic. In less than three years, in May 1916, the office was moved to Waverley Station with new telephone equipment. A *Railway Magazine* article in 1920 said tactfully of the Portobello office 'The equipment then installed, while it covered its purpose, was found somewhat unsuitable for development'. Other offices were opened at Coatbridge, for the Western Division, in August 1914 and at Burntisland, for the Northern Division, in November 1920.

At Waverley the Southern District control covered the old Southern and Central Divisions combined, the previous areas being:

Southern Division – Carlisle to Kilnknowe Junction and all branches south of Galashiels.

Central Division – North of Kilnknowe Junction and Berwick to Ratho and Dalmeny.

The North British control system concentrated on the actual movement of trains rather than on the relief and utilisation of train crews. The tight timetabling and defined traincrew workings that were a notable feature of the 1951 Waverley route operation probably owed much to this tradition of well controlled movements of goods trains.

Towards the end of the life of the Waverley route, modernisation arrived in the shape of Millerhill Yard which was opened in 1962. At the southern end of the route a connection was provided to the new yard at Kingmoor which was intended to rationalise the handling of goods traffic at Carlisle. The improved terminal facilities gave the line a potential handling capacity that far exceeded the traffic then offering. But in 1951 opposite conditions prevailed, 14 up and 15 down through goods trains being dealt with daily at the old yards at each end of the route.

The goods traffic very largely consisted of these through workings. Traffic originating on the route was small apart from the output of the Lothian coalfield which mostly involved only short hauls, at least as far as the Waverley route was concerned. The towns of Hawick and Galashiels, with their tweed mills, had some demand for coal but their outward traffic was small. Even in 1920, with negligible road competition, receipts for passenger and goods traffic at these and other stations were approximately equal. Through traffic built up as it doubtless suited the NBR to despatch what English traffic it could via the Waverley route in preference to the East Coast, an additional 40 miles of its own haulage being obtained thereby before handing over to a foreign company at Carlisle. Some of the 1951 traffic pattern is probably attributable to a survival of this policy. There is also the possibility that congestion on the route over Beattock had led to some post-nationalisation diversion. Although a memory of the past by 1951, mention must be made of the through Edinburgh to Newcastle workings via Riccarton Junction and the Border Counties Railway, an unlikely route which, however, again gave the North British a larger share of the mileage.

At Carlisle all goods traffic from the Hawick direction was routed to the ex-North British Canal Yard. Transfer

V2 No. 60823, assisted in the rear by J36 No. 65259, on the 9.0 a.m. Carlisle Canal to Portobello, approaching Riccarton Junction on 19th September 1953.

AUTHOR'S COLLECTION

A Class E goods on the final climb at 1 in 75 from Shankend to Whitrope summit, headed by B1 No. 61351 on 30th May 1961. J. F. AYLARD

V2 No. 60819 with the 12.30 p.m. Class E goods from Carlisle Canal to Niddrie West Yard at Shankend on 30th May 1961. J. F. AYLARD

workings were required to the various yards that were at one time the property of other pre-grouping companies that worked into Carlisle. At the Edinburgh end the majority of through goods trains were worked into Niddrie West Yard on the Edinburgh Suburban line adjacent to Niddrie West Junction. Traffic to and from this yard could avoid Waverley station by using the Suburban line and the spur to Haymarket West Junction. In describing the timetable in detail, frequent reference will be made to these two yards and for convenience unqualified reference hereafter to Canal and Niddrie yards should be taken as meaning Carlisle Canal Yard and Niddrie West Yard respectively. In the down direction ten out of fifteen goods trains from Carlisle were routed to Niddrie. Of the remaining five, three terminated at Portobello and two at Meadows Yard. Eight out of fourteen up trains originated at Niddrie, three at Haymarket, one at Waverley station and two at Portobello. 'Originated' in this context means that the trains commenced their journey over the Waverley route as some loads were worked through from north of Edinburgh. Locomotives and crews would, however, be changed in all cases at the yards indicated. In most cases Hawick was a convenient mid-journey stop for water and for crew changing. The practice of crew changeovers between specified trains was prevalent on the Waverley route and the arrangements are detailed separately in *Table 4*. Some protracted booked stops at Hawick were

TABLE 4

TRAIN CREW WORKINGS - WAVERLEY ROUTE

Summer 1951

CARLISLE CREWS

OUT													
	Train	528	618	567	656	503	600	772	626	594	504	617	529
	Class	E	E	E	E	E	E	E	E	E	H	E	E
		a.m.	a.m.	a.m.	a.m.	a.m.	a.m.	a.m.	p.m.	p.m.	p.m.	p.m.	p.m.
Canal Yard	dep	12.20	2.15	3.15	5.50	8.0	10.40	11.35	12.35	2.35	4.0	8.45	10.0
Hawick	arr	3.17	4.22	6.55	8.17	9.54	12.38	1.43	3.13	4.42	6.50	10.52	-
St. Boswells	arr	-	-	-	-	-	-	-	-	-	-	-	1.49
		a.m.	a.m.	a.m.	a.m.	a.m.	p.m.	p.m.	p.m.	p.m.	p.m.	a.m.	p.m.
St. Boswells	dep	-	-	-	-	-	-	-	-	-	-	-	2.25
Hawick	dep	3.55	4.35	7.5	9.5	10.20	1.42	2.10	4.45	6.5	7.35	12.15	-
Canal Yard	arr	5.19	5.56	8.26	10.59	12.14	3.39	4.4	6.39	8.26	9.29	2.4	4.4
RETURN	*Train*	569	509	577	626	651	525	539	500	537	517	558	625
	Class	C	C	C	E	E	E	E	E	H	E	E	C

EDINBURGH CREWS

OUT																	
	Train	625	569	509	522	577	626	651	525	539	500	537	517	240	558	575	557
	Class	C	C	C	F	C	E	E	E	E	E	H	E	B	E	C	C
		a.m.	a.m.	a.m.	a.m.	a.m.	a.m.	a.m.	a.m.	a.m.	p.m.	p.m.	p.m.	p.m.	p.m.	p.m.	p.m.
Haymarket	dep	12.30	-	-	-	-	5.35	-	-	-	-	-	-	-	-	7.55	-
Waverley	dep	-	-	-	-	-	-	-	-	-	-	-	-	7.2	-	-	8.50
Portobello	dep	-	-	-	2.25	-	-	-	10.30	-	-	-	-	-	7.25	-	-
Niddrie W. Yard	dep	-	1.45	2.20	-	4.50	-	7.30	-	11.0	1.30	2.55	4.40	-	-	-	-
St. Boswells	arr	2.9	-	-	-	-	-	-	-	-	-	-	-	-	-	-	-
Hawick	arr	-	3.28	4.2	5.33	6.35	8.3	9.36	12.44	1.52	3.37	5.30	6.46	8.53	10.54	-	-
Canal Yard	arr	-	-	-	-	-	-	-	-	-	-	-	-	-	-	11.41	12.6
		a.m.	a.m.	a.m.	a.m.	a.m.	a.m.	a.m.	p.m.	p.m.	p.m.	p.m.	p.m.	p.m.	p.m.	a.m.	a.m.
Canal Yard	dep	-	-	-	-	-	-	-	-	-	-	-	-	-	-	1.10	1.30
Hawick	dep	-	3.50	4.42	6.21	7.25	8.35	10.15	1.20	2.10	3.50	6.5	7.15	9.29	11.15	-	-
St. Boswells	dep	2.20	-	-	-	-	-	-	-	-	-	-	-	-	-	-	-
Niddrie W. Yard	arr	-	5.54	6.41	-	9.29	10.40	12.2	3.26	4.46	-	-	9.50	11.33	1.19	4.12	4.32
Portobello	arr	4.2	-	-	-	-	-	-	-	-	6.3	-	-	-	-	-	-
Meadows Yard	arr	-	-	-	-	-	-	-	-	-	-	8.25	-	-	-	-	-
Waverley	arr	-	-	-	7.49	-	-	-	-	-	-	-	-	-	-	-	-
RETURN	*Train*	529	528	618	185	567	656	503	600	772	626	594	504	612	617	768	767
	Class	E	E	E	A	E	E	D	E	E	E	E	H	E	E	C	C

TABLE 5

THROUGH GOODS TRAINS - WAVERLEY ROUTE

Tuesdays to Fridays, Summer 1951

Distance M.C	**DOWN**																
		Train No.	528	768	767	618	567	656	503	600	772	626	594	504	612	617	529
		Class	E	C	C	C	E	E	D	E	E	E	E	H	E	E	E
			a.m.	a.m.	a.m.	a.m.	a.m.	a.m.	a.m.	a.m.	a.m.	p.m.	p.m.	p.m.	p.m.	p.m.	p.m.
00.00	Carlisle Canal Yard	dep	12.20	1.10	1.30	2.15	3.15	5.50	8.0	10.40	11.35	12.35	2.35	4.0	5.50	8.45	10.0
23.21	Newcastleton	pass	1.7	1.48	2.8	3.9B	4.2	6.49B	8.50B	11.27	12.30B	1.22	3.29B	5.26B	6.44B	9.39B	10.54B
31.31	Riccarton Jcn.	pass	1.42	2.9	2.29	3.47	5.2	7.27	9.23	12.2	1.7	2.35	4.7	6.12	7.22	10.17	11.32
33.43	Whitrope	pass	1.50	2.15	2.36	3.55	5.13	7.35	9.30	12.10	1.15	2.46	4.15	6.22	7.30	10.25	11.40
41.71	Stobs Camp	pass	3.6	-	-	-	6.45	8.7	-	-	-	-	-	-	-	-	-
44.31	Hawick	arr	3.17	2.34	2.54	4.22	6.55	8.17	9.54	12.38	1.43	3.13	4.42	6.56	7.57	10.52	12.7
		dep	3.50	2.45	3.5	4.42	7.25	8.35	10.15	1.20	2.10	3.50	6.5	7.15	9.29	11.15	1.20
56.53	St. Boswells	arr	pass	pass	pass	pass	pass	pass	pass	pass	pass	pass	pass	pass	pass	pass	1.49
		dep	4.17	3.6	3.26	5.9	7.52	9.2	10.38	1.47	2.37	4.71	6.32	7.51	9.56	11.42	2.20
63.55	Galashiels	pass	4.31	3.16	3.36	5.23	8.6	9.16	10.50	2.1	2.51	4.31	6.46	8.7	10.10	11.56	2.37
79.22	Falahill	pass	5.16	3.46	4.6	6.8	8.51	10.1	11.30	2.46	4.5	5.16	7.31	9.2	10.55	12.41	3.22
88.77	Hardengreen Jcn.	pass	5.41	4.1	4.21	6.33	9.16	10.26	11.50	3.13	4.33	5.41	7.56	9.34	11.20	1.6	3.47
92.65	Niddrie South Jcn.	pass	5.49	4.7	4.27	6.41	9.24	10.34	11.57	3.21	4.41	5.50	8.7	9.44	11.28	1.14	3.55
93.44	Niddrie West Yard	arr	5.54	4.12	4.33	-	-	10.40	12.2	3.26	4.46	-	-	9.50	11.33	1.19	-
94.18	Portobello	arr				-	9.29					6.3	-				4.2
95.10	Meadows Yard	arr				6.55							8.25				

Distance M.C	**UP**															
		Train No.	625	569	509	577	626	651	525	539	500	537	517	558	575	557
		Class	C	C	C	C	E	E	E	E	E	H	E	E	C	C
			a.m.	a.m.	a.m.	a.m.	a.m.	a.m.	a.m.	a.m.	p.m.	p.m.	p.m.	p.m.	p.m.	p.m.
-- --	Haymarket Goods	dep	12.30				5.35								7.55	
00.00	Edinburgh Waverley	dep	pass				pass								pass	8.50
03.00	Portobello	dep	pass				pass		10.30					7.25	pass	pass
-- --	Niddrie West Yard	dep	-	1.45	2.20	4.50	-	7.30	-	11.0	1.30	2.55	4.40	-	-	-
04.33	Niddrie South Jcn.	pass	12.48	1.48	2.23	4.55	5.59	7.33	10.40	11.4	1.33	2.59	4.43	7.34	8.14	9.1
08.21	Hardengreen Jcn.	arr	12.56	1.56	2.31	5.1	6.9	7.43	10.50	11.15	1.43	3.12	4.53	7.44	8.22	pass
		dep	1.1B	2.2B	2.36B	5.8B	6.15B	7.48B	10.56B	11.20B	1.48B	3.17B	4.58B	7.50B	8.35B	9.7
17.76	Falahill	pass	1.37	2.38	3.12	5.44	6.58	8.31	11.39	12.3	2.32	4.10	5.41	8.35	9.11	9.41
33.43	Galashiels	pass	1.57	2.58	3.32	6.4	7.24	8.57	12.5	12.29	2.58	4.42	6.7	8.59	9.31	10.2
40.65	St. Boswells	arr	2.9	pass	pass	pass	pass	pass	pass	12.44	pass	pass	pass	9.14	pass	pass
		dep	2.25	3.8	3.42	6.14	7.37	9.10	12.18	1.23	3.11	4.59	6.20	10.25	9.41	10.12
52.67	Hawick	arr	pass	3.28	4.2	6.35	8.3	9.36	12.44	1.52	3.37	5.30	6.46	10.54	10.1	10.32
		dep	2.46	3.55	4.35B	7.5B	9.5B	10.20B	1.42B	2.10B	4.45B	6.5B	7.35B	12.15B	10.20B	10.42
65.68	Riccarton Jcn.	pass	3.21	4.33	5.13	7.43	10.3	11.18	2.40	3.8	5.43	7.13	8.47	1.8	10.58	11.23
97.18	Carlisle Canal Yard	arr	4.4	5.19	5.56	8.27	10.59	12.14	3.39	4.4	6.39	8.26	9.29	2.4	11.41	12.6

NOTE: B — Departure time with banking assistance

0.00 — Stands for other trains to pass or clear section

K2 No. 4986, fitted with a side window cab, heading a No. 1 express goods at Thornton Junction in 1939. S. H. FREESE

due to the necessity of waiting for the arrival of the designated 'changeover' train in the opposite direction.

Practically all of the full range of the very detailed British Rail classification of trains was involved in the Waverley route traffic. This classification is given in full in *Appendix* 2. A simplified timetable for the through goods trains in midweek is shown in *Table* 5. In the down direction there were two Class C trains, Nos. 768 and 767, which left Canal at 1.10 a.m. and 1.30 a.m. respectively and maintained an unvarying 20 minutes separation to Niddrie. No. 768 continued from Niddrie at 5.5 a.m. to Dundee, arriving 7.30 a.m. No. 767 followed at 5.20 a.m. and finished its journey at Perth at 7.20 p.m. The Class C timing of 3 hours 2 minutes from Canal to Niddrie may be compared with the 2 hours 39 minutes then allowed between Carlisle Citadel and Edinburgh Waverley for the 8.50 a.m. ex-St. Pancras, the small difference illustrating the unsuitability of the route for express running. Incidentally the fastest booking from Carlisle to Edinburgh in the 1951 WTT was that of the 12.7 a.m. Sunday newspaper train from Carlisle (9.27 p.m. Saturdays from Manchester Victoria) which stopped only at Hawick and reached Waverley at 2.40 a.m. Another Perth load was conveyed by the 8.40 a.m. Class D from Canal. This train was banked at Newcastleton and made Niddrie in just over 4 hours. Perth was eventually reached at 5.10 p.m.

There were eleven Class E trains through from Carlisle to Edinburgh. Eight of these carried loads which were remarshalled at Edinburgh yards. The first, 12.20 a.m. from Canal to Niddrie, spent nearly one hour in the refuge siding at Stobs Camp where it was passed by the two Class C trains mentioned above. Niddrie loads were also conveyed from Canal by Nos. 600 and 607 at 10.45 a.m. and 8.45 p.m. respectively. Two trains ran through to Meadows Yard, Nos. 618 and 594, the 2.15 a.m. and 2.35 p.m. from Canal. In 1951, these were the only two booked workings over the portion of the Lothian Lines between Niddrie South and Niddrie North Junctions. There were no movements in the opposite direction. The no-token system avoided complications due to such unbalanced workings in single lines. The traffic density on the Niddrie South to North Junction link was not typical of the contemporary use made of the Lothian Lines; some sixteen trains in all were booked daily to converge in the down direction at Niddrie North

J35 No. 9363 banking a long coal train hauled by J38 No. 1424 at Thornton Junction in 1939. S. H. FREESE

Ex-NBR D31 No. 9740 at Kittybrewster in July 1919. This engine was transferred to the GN of S section in 1926 where it remained until withdrawal in 1947. S. H. FREESE

St. Boswells shed was adjacent to the station. A J35 was the resident on 16th July 1954.
A. R. GOULT

Junction. Good time-keeping was required from No. 618 as Niddrie South Junction was booked to be passed at 6.41 a.m., only six minutes in advance of No. 253, the Class A down Postal, 4.8 a.m. ex-Carlisle Citadel. Three trains ran from Canal to Portobello, No. 567 at 3.15 a.m. was looped at Riccarton Junction to allow No. 253 Postal to pass. Ten miles later it was put into the refuge at Stobs Camp, the last block post before Hawick, to be passed by the 9.5 p.m. St. Pancras to Edinburgh sleeper. After the sleeper had been dealt with at Hawick, the down platform was occupied by the stock of the 6.40 a.m. Class B to Waverley, and until the latter had departed No. 567 could not be accepted at Hawick South box. Booked departure from Stobs Camp was therefore 6.45 a.m. and so nearly 3 hours were spent between Newcastleton and Hawick. No. 626, the 12.35 p.m. from Canal was looped at Riccarton to be passed by the 1.26 p.m. Class A from Carlisle. The third Portobello train No. 529, 10.0 p.m. from Canal, was unusual in changing crews at St. Boswells, this after a stop of 1 hour 13 minutes at Hawick.

The remaining three down Class E trains from Canal ran to Niddrie with loads destined for Aberdeen yards, No. 656 at 5.50 a.m. for Craiginches and Nos. 722 and 612 at 11.35 a.m. and 5.50 p.m. for Kittybrewster. The 5.50 a.m. was booked to wait at Stobs Camp until the 8.7 a.m. Class A Hawick to Waverley had started its journey and No. 722 was shunted to Falahill for the 1.26 p.m. from Carlisle to pass. All three trains were marshalled in the same order:

1. GND fitted
2. Aberdeen fitted
3. Aberdeen unfitted
4. GNS unfitted

The remaining through train from Canal was the 4.0 p.m. Class H No. 504. With banking assistance from Newcastleton and a shortish stop at Hawick, Niddrie was reached in 5 hours and 50 minutes, a better time than that made by some of the Class E trains.

The down stopping goods train ran to or from St. Boswells or Hawick. No. 13 down, the 7.0 a.m. Class K from Canal stopped at Longtown, Newcastleton, Riccarton Junction, Shankend and Stobs en route to Hawick. No times were specified after the departure from Canal. At 8.45 a.m. a Class H train, No. 558, left St. Boswells for Portobello. After its first stop at Galashiels it followed No. 656 and made further calls at Falahill and Hardengreen Junction. No. 569 was the untimed return working of the 9.0 a.m. Class K from Hardengreen Junction to Galashiels. Stops were made at all intermediate yards. A further Class K train, No. 21, left Canal at 9.45 a.m. stopping at all stations to Riccarton Junction where the arrival time was 2.0 p.m. Another stopping goods, No. 521 Class H, left Hawick at 11.45 a.m. for Niddrie, arriving 3.38 p.m. after calling at St. Boswells, Galashiels, Falahill and Hardengreen Junction.

The evening down stopping goods included a Class E train, No. 506 at 6.40 p.m. from Hawick, calling only at St. Boswells en route to Portobello. A note for this train stated 'Cadder traffic to be sectionised and placed next engine'. At St. Boswells, traffic from Hawick to the north via Niddrie was also detached to await the 8.55 p.m. and in exchange traffic for Cadder from Kelso, Jedburgh and Galashiels (sic) was attached.

The 8.55 p.m. Class J, No. 775 from St. Boswells was marshalled as follows:

1. Traffic to be detached at Hardengreen
2. Livestock for west of Ratho
3. Livestock for suburban stations and north of Forth Bridge
4. Niddrie traffic, suburban and north of Forth Bridge

At Galashiels, No. 775 was passed by the 7.33 p.m. Class A from Carlisle and then made Hardengreen in time for the 5.50 p.m. Class E from Canal to pass. The final daily down train to be mentioned was the 11.15 p.m. Class F from Canal to St. Boswells stopping only at Hawick. A note for this train stated that the single engine load was not to be exceeded.

On Tuesdays, Gorgie market, which also generated cattle traffic on the branches, had a special arranged by Control from Hassendean, Belses, Bowland, Stow and stations up to Gorebridge. For St. Boswells sales on Mondays an engine and van were provided at 12.0 noon from Hawick to work as required. The Thursday sale at Longtown also required an engine and van from Canal to work back loaded livestock.

In the up direction six Class C trains ran daily compared with two northbound although there was a corresponding reduction in up Class E trains. It is possible that marshalling arrangements produced a better distribution of fitted wagons southbound. Three of the Class C trains commenced their Waverley route journey at Niddrie, all in the early morning. No. 569 at 1.45 a.m. was the 8.20 p.m. from Aberdeen. This train was followed by No. 509 at 2.20 a.m. which originated at Inverkeithing at 12.20 a.m. Finally, No. 577 at 4.50 a.m. was the continuation of the 10.25 p.m. from Aberdeen. This train continued from Canal to Upperby with a full load for the LNW. Nos. 569 and 509 were both marshalled: 1 – Midland, 2 – LNW, 3 – Carlisle. No. 569 additionally conveyed a Crown Street shed wagon next to the engine.

Two further Class C trains, both from Dundee, ran through to Canal from Haymarket via Waverley station. These left Haymarkey at 12.30 a.m. (No. 625) and 7.35 p.m. (No. 575) and were the 9.50 p.m. and 3.55 p.m. respectively from Dundee, No. 625 stopped at St. Boswells for its crew changeover and was unique in being booked to pass Hawick without stopping. The sixth Class C train was the 8.50 p.m. from Waverley, No. 587. This was the only through goods which was not banked from Hardengreen to Falahill. Marshalling arrangements for Nos. 625, 575 and 557 were similar to those for No. 509.

Of the seven up Class E trains, four commenced at Niddrie. These were day trains, the first being No. 651 at 7.30 a.m., a continuation of the 12.30 a.m. from Dundee. No indication of marshalling was given for this train but No. 539 at 11.0 a.m. from Niddrie, the 1.0 a.m. from Aberdeen Craiginches, was marshalled: 1 – Carlisle, 2 – NE via Carlisle, 3 – Midland, 4 – LNW. No. 539 was shunted at St. Boswells to be passed by the 12.5 p.m. Class A ex-Waverley. No. 500 at 1.30 p.m. and No. 517 at 4.40 p.m. were made up at Niddrie and were noted as 'Load to be arranged'.

Haymarkey despatched a Class E train, No. 626 at 5.35 a.m., the continuation of the 12.15 a.m. from Perth. Marshalling was: 1 – LNW, 2 – Midland, 3 – Carlisle. The two remaining Class E workings commenced at Portobello, No. 525 at 10.30 a.m. and No. 558 at 7.25 p.m. No. details of the origin or destination of the loads were specified. The same was the case with the solitary Class H through train, No. 537 at 2.55 p.m. from Niddrie.

A feature of the up timetable was that through goods trains were so well dovetailed with the passenger service that all overtaking took place during the stops for water and remanning at Hawick with the sole exception already mentioned of the shunting of No. 539 at St. Boswells.

The up stopping goods service commenced with the 1.0 a.m. Class J from Niddrie to St. Boswells, No. 560 which was shunted at Falahill for No. 569 to pass. The only traffic stop was made at Galashiels. Two following trains started from Portobello, the 2.25 a.m. Class F to Hawick, No. 522, and the 5.20 a.m. Class H to St. Boswells, No. 523. No. 522 called at Galashiels to leave off only and took Kelso branch and Melrose traffic to St. Boswells. No. 523 called conditionally at Galashiels. When the stop was made it followed No. 626 from Galashiels to St. Boswells. No. 524 left Hardengreen Junction for Galashiels at 9.0 a.m. and thereafter made untimed calls at all intermediate yards. Further south, all yards between Hawick and Carlisle were served by Class K No. 108, the untimed return working of No. 13 down. In the evening two further Class H local goods ran in the up direction. These were No. 86 at 7.17 p.m. from St. Boswells to Canal and No. 502 at 11.15 p.m. from Falahill to Hawick. No. 86 called at Hawick and Riccarton Junction and No. 502 at St. Boswells. Melrose was served from St. Boswells by a booked return trip in the middle of the day and the St. Boswells pilot also made a return trip as far as Hassendean when required.

Two of the stopping goods, the 7.0 a.m. Canal to Hawick and return and the 9.0 a.m. Hardengreen to Galashiels were 'Bonus' workings. The crews earned bonus money in accordance with the work done and the speed of doing it. An engineman recalled the return Hawick job being done from Canal in 6 to 6½ hours. The fireman jumped off to change points and assisted the guard as much as possible while shunting; the driver looked after the fire and water level.

The Lothian coalfield was completely different in character, both in environment and traffic, from the rest of the route. Much of the short trip traffic was done by St. Margaret's engines based on the Portobello yards. Except for this traffic, the requirement for shunting and pilot engines was comparatively small. Hardengreen Junction, however, was provided with four pilot and shunting engines throughout the 24 hours, three of which were classified PG&M (passenger, goods and mineral), thus ensuring that all classes of train could be banked to Falahill as required. Lothian coal going south by the Waverley route was tripped to Falahill for attachment there in order to ease loads up the bank. Galashiels had a passenger and goods pilot available daily from 5.30 a.m. to 9.0 p.m. Riccarton had two goods pilots, one with an eight hour shift from 9.0 p.m. to 5.0 a.m. and the second covering 5.15 a.m. to 7.15 p.m. Both had duties defined as 'shunting and assisting'.

The working of the northern branches was not fully defined in the WTT as many short trip workings to colliery sidings were made 'as required'. A single shift from Portobello was, however, booked to work up the Glencorse branch, leaving Portobello at 8.45 a.m. and arriving back at 4.5 p.m. The Polton branch was similarly worked and in addition the branch passenger engine was available for goods working during its spare time at Polton. The Penicuik and Dalkeith branches both had two booked Class K trains from Hardengreen Junction daily.

The first train of the day up the long branch to Galashiels via Peebles was the 6.0 a.m. Class K, No. 695 from Hardengren Junction to Peebles. This returned untimed, still as No. 695, to Hardengreen. On Tuesdays only the return journey was extended to Gorgie with livestock for the cattle market from all stations from Peebles to Millerhill. A down Class K working originated at Peebles at 3.0 p.m., returning from Hardengreen at 7.0. p.m. If braked traffic for King's Cross was conveyed, the train ran through to Niddrie, the engine and brake van returning thence at 6.17 p.m. to pick up its working from Hardengreen. Another Peebles shift commenced at 8.30 a.m. to work the 9.20 a.m. Class K to Galashiels, leaving there on the return trip at 12.15 p.m. Galashiels was required to provide a fresh engine for the 12.15 p.m. working. On Tuesdays the demands of traffic for Gorgie market were met by this crew turning out at 6.40 a.m. to make a conditional trip to Walkerburn, returning with cattle picked up there and also at Innerleithan and Cardrona. When this train ran, the Hardengreen crew of No .695 were enjoined to assist at Peebles in making up the 9.20 a.m.

Although the Lauder Light Railway lost its passenger service as long ago as 1932, it was still provided with tablet facilities from Fountainhill to Oxton. The final section from Oxton to Lauder was worked as 'one engine in steam'. One Class K train ran daily through from Galashiels, leaving at 9.29 a.m. with a return arrival at 1.40 p.m. The Galashiels to Selkirk branch had the remarkable timetable shown in *Table 6.* Only one return passenger trip survived and the first Class K train preceded the outward passenger by a fairly close margin. As soon as the return passenger train had surrendered its tablet at Galashiels the return Class K working commenced. After this rush of business there was no other traffic except the afternoon Class K working. Selkirk signal box was officially opened from 6.15 a.m. to 5.0 p.m., although nearly five hours elapsed in the middle of this period without a train on the branch. Incidentally, the 8.20 a.m. Class B from Selkirk made a reasonable connection into the 8.44 a.m. to Waverley at Galashiels. With no return service it is little wonder that passenger facilities were withdrawn from the branch on 10th September 1951 at the end of the currency of the timetable under discussion.

TABLE 6
SELKIRK BRANCH Working Timetable, Summer 1951

Distance M.C.	**UP**	*Train No. / Class*	500 K	368 B	534 K (SX)
			a.m.	a.m.	p.m.
0.00	Galashiels	dep	6.40	7.57	1.55
0.78	Selkirk Jcn.	pass	-	(7.59)	(1.59)
4.09	Lindean	dep	-	8.7	2.13
6.12	Selkirk	arr	7.30	8.13	2.25

NOTES No.500 Up train works Gas Works Siding and Lindean as required.

Distance M.C.	**DOWN**	*Train No. / Class*	220 B	368 K	534 K (SX)
			a.m.	a.m.	p.m.
0.00	Selkirk	dep	8.20	8.35	4.25
2.03	Lindean	dep	8.26	-	4.40
5.14	Selkirk Jcn.	pass	(8.33)	-	(4.50)
6.12	Galashiels	arr	8.35	9.0	4.55

NOTES No.500 Down train works Lindean and Gas Works Siding as required.
No.774 engine, guard and van to make trip at 5.45 p.m. Galashiels to St. Boswells with South traffic. Works back as required.

SIDINGS Galafoot Gas Works; Netherdale Mill; Galashiels Electric; Ettrick Mill; St. Mary's Mill.

The branch from St. Boswells through Duns to Reston had suffered permanent damage from flooding during the storm of 12th August 1948. A service of both passenger and goods trains remained between Reston and Duns but from the St. Boswells end operation was confined to a morning Class K return trip to Greenlaw.

The Kelso and Tweedmouth branch from St. Boswells was comparatively busy with five passenger workings in each direction and two Class K trains from St. Boswells to Kelso. Both of these broke their return journeys at Roxburgh to make a return trip on the Jedburgh branch. There was also a Class H train 1.0 p.m. from Tweedmouth to Kelso, Roxburgh and St. Boswells arriving at 4.1 p.m. The return departure was at 5.20 p.m. calling only at Kelso and reaching Tweedmouth at 8.1 p.m.

The Langholm branch was served by a Class K train which left Canal at 5.35 a.m. The first up passenger from Langholm at 7.13 a.m. ran as a mixed train to Riddings Junction with conditional increases in timing when intermediate attachments were made. A further return Class K trip was made from Langholm at 11.30 a.m. to Riddings Junction. After a quick turn round, the return arrival was at 12.38 p.m.

The one-time Border Counties Railway from Riccarton Junction to Reedsmouth and Hexham was not covered by the Edinburgh District WTT. The sole reference to goods traffic was a note of the departure of a Class K goods from Riccarton to Reedsmouth at 7.0 a.m.

Finally, mention must be made of the one daily trip on the Longtown to Gretna branch, a Class H leaving Canal at 12.15 p.m. and arriving back at 7.7 p.m.

The transformation which has taken place between 1951 and the present day is an object lesson in transport history. Gone are the special trains on Tuesdays to satisfy the requirements of Gorgie market and long forgotten are the carefully mentioned connections between the stopping goods on remote branches and the long distance trains to London. In 1969 a through rail route which probably transported some 7,000 tons of goods and minerals throughout its length each day completely disappeared. In view of its notorious difficulty of operation, the elimination of the Waverley route as a trunk line for long distance traffic was possibly to be expected in an era of declining rail usage. The logical extension of a transport policy which concentrated rail capacity on long-haul traffic was that the retention of the line to serve the comparatively small intermediate towns was not justified. So virtually the whole area previously served by the route is now without railways.

Sources

John Thomas: *A Regional History of the Railways of Great Britain, Vol. VI, Scotland: The Lowlands and Borders.* David and Charles.

British Railways: Scottish Region; Working Time Table, Edinburgh District. Summer 1951.

J37 No. 64614 with a brake van alongside Piershill Junction box, Edinburgh, on 4th June 1963. R. F. ORPWOOD

CHAPTER FOUR

THE GREAT EASTERN SECTION AT ELY AND ST. IVES

J20 No. 8276 with an up coal train at Shelford in 1932. Seventeen miles of mostly adverse gradients lay ahead.
LOCOMOTIVE PUBLISHING CO.

THE Great Eastern Railway served a primarily agricultural community outside the London area. In contrast to other lines from London to districts north of the Thames, no large centres of industry existed within its territory. It is, therefore, not surprising that the gross receipts from passengers, swollen by the enormous London suburban traffic, exceeded those for goods. The figures for 1913, the last year of the GER unaffected by the Great War and its aftermath, are £3,239,036 and £2,703,173 respectively. The goods receipts resulted from a total tonnage conveyed of 13,232,507 made up by 5,717,841 tons of merchandise and 7,514,666 tons of minerals.

There is ample evidence of both Great Eastern and, later, LNER enterprise in providing facilities for handling goods traffic. In addition to the well known LNER developments at Whitemoor which are referred to later, the inauguration in 1924 of the Harwich to Zeebrugge train ferry jointly by Great Eastern Train Ferries Ltd. and La Société Belgo-Anglaise des Ferry Boats provided a useful and long-lived service. Three war surplus train ferries and the redundant train ferry berth at Southampton, which was re-erected at Harwich, were all put to good use. On a smaller scale, but no less significant, was the installation in 1898 of Britain's first power signalling system on the goods lines at Granary Junction, Bishopsgate. This was an electro-pneumatic point control and interlocking apparatus supplied by McKenzie and Holland Ltd. In the same year construction of the Whitechapel wagon hoist commenced. This enabled wagons to be transferred from the Great Eastern to the East London line 46 feet below and avoided the awkward reversal at East London Junction. The capacity of the hoist was two loaded wagons with a total weight of 35 tons.

There was a sizeable flow of merchandise traffic along the Colchester main line from London. However, much of the Great Eastern goods traffic entered the system at Peterborough or March. Peterborough was the point where originally the Great Northern, London and North Western and Midland railways all handed over goods to the GER which had sorting sidings at Stanground yard and at Whittlesea. The large amount of trip traffic between the yards of the various railways resulted in persistent local congestion. Various attempts by the Great Eastern to secure direct access to the South Yorkshire coalfields eventually bore fruit in 1879 when the Great Northern entered into an agreement for the GN and GE Joint line which effectively formed a direct link between March and Doncaster. The agreement brought greater advantage to the Great Eastern than to the Great Northern. The co-operation of the latter was due to the recognition that the only alternative would inevitably be acquisition by the Great Eastern of an independent line to the coalfields.

From the completion of the GN and GE Joint line in 1882 the existing coal traffic from Peterborough to London via Cambridge was greatly augmented by a flow from March. The predominance of minerals in the goods tonnage is thereby explained. The Great Eastern expanded the facilities at March by opening marshalling

Wagons running down the hump to the marshalling sidings at Whitemoor up yard. LNER

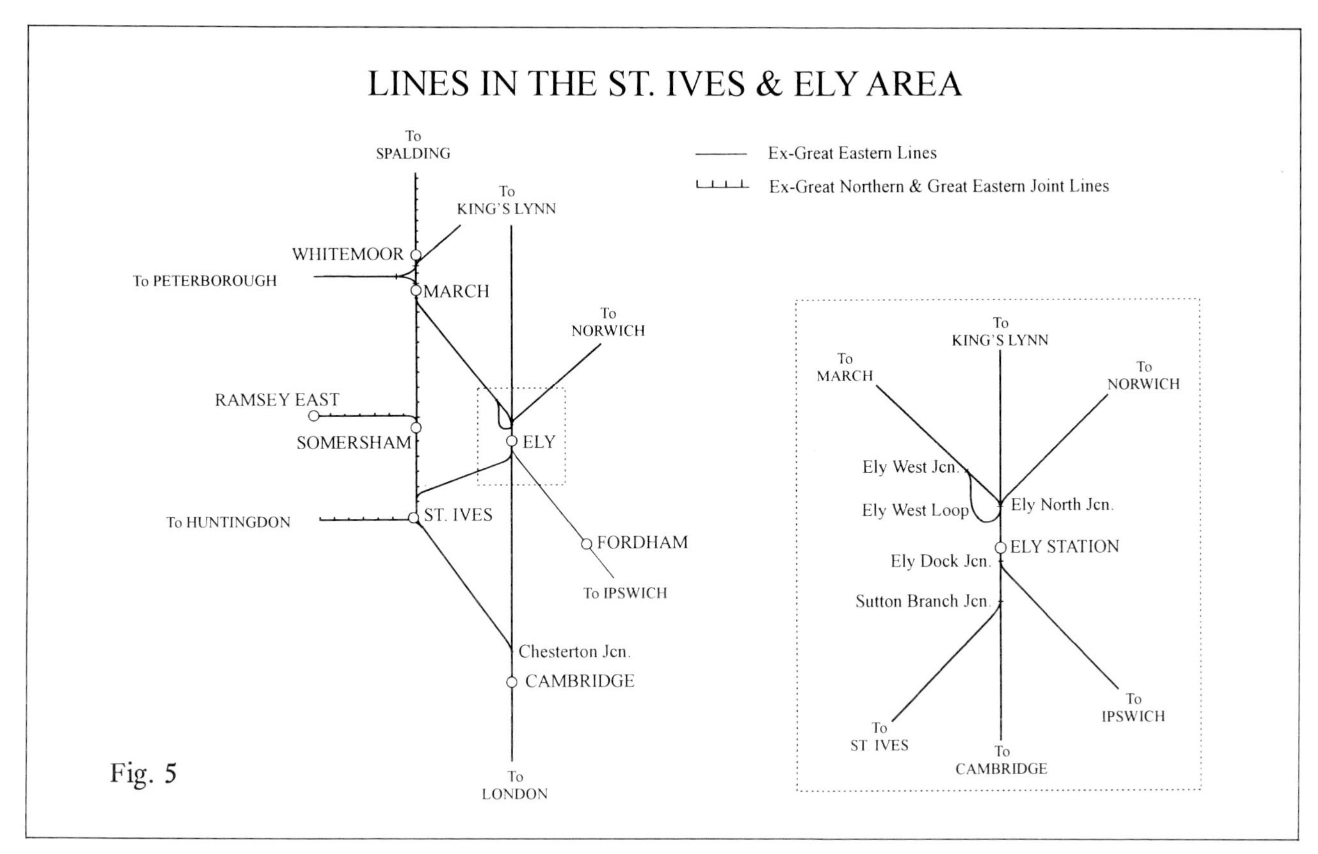

Fig. 5

yards at Whitemoor, a mile or so to the north. Despite the opening in 1909 of a new up yard to hold 1,500 wagons, at which time some 100 engines were shedded at March, the Peterborough traffic still remained significant until the revolution effected at Whitemoor by the LNER in 1929 with the opening of the new up gravity yard, equipped with the first rail retarders in Great Britain. This was followed by the corresponding down yard in 1933. Thereafter the traffic exchanged at Peterborough decreased to such an extent that Peterborough East shed was closed in 1939. Fortunately, a Working Time Table for the summer of 1927 is available to enable a survey to be made of an LNER traffic pattern that was virtually unaltered from GER days. In order to include trains using the Cambridge main line from London to King's Lynn and Norwich, the focal points of Ely and St. Ives have been chosen for detailed consideration.

A diagram of the railways in the Ely and St. Ives district, with an inset detailing the junctions at Ely, is given in *Fig.* 5. The rail map of today shows that Ely is still a junction of important routes, only the branch to St. Ives via Sutton having been closed. St. Ives, however, has disappeared completely from the railway scene. In 1927 large proportion of the goods traffic to and from East Anglia passed through Ely North Junction, the chief exception being those trains between London and March which travelled via St. Ives and, of course, the traffic on the Colchester main line.

The main line from London to Norwich via Colchester was completed in 1849, only four years after the commencement of through traffic on the Eastern Counties line via Cambridge and Ely. Tradition persisted, however, and a proportion of the London goods traffic to Norwich and beyond used the Ely route in LNER days. Over half of the London to Peterborough East or Whitemoor trains used the St. Ives route but all King's Lynn trains travelled via Ely. Other main traffic flows through Ely North Junction consisted of trains from the March line to Ipswich via Ely Dock Junction and Bury St. Edmunds and to the Norwich district via Ely West Curve. The West Curve was opened on 1st October 1890 to permit trains to run direct from March to Norwich. The unusual loop arrangement avoided the necessity of bridging both the Lynn line and the River Ouse but it did, however, add to the concentration of traffic at the North Junction.

In contrast to Ely, main line goods traffic at St. Ives was practically limited to London trains to and from Peterborough East and Whitemoor. There was, however, considerable variety in the branch traffic, both the Great Northern section and the Midland division of the LMS being involved. North of Needingworth Junction, where the branch through Sutton to Ely diverged, the original Eastern Counties line to March was incorporated into the GN and GE Joint lines as also was the branch from St. Ives to Huntington. From the Great Northern point of

O4 No. 3692 with a lengthy goods train at Pyewipe Junction, Lincoln, on 19th April 1947. H. C. CASSERLEY

view, the only potential benefit to be gained from joint ownership of these lines was their use for through traffic to and from the south. Although the necessary junction existed between the main line and the branch at Huntington, this use would have required some upgrading of the branch and the provision of a west to north curve at St. Ives to permit through running. The curve was intended but never constructed. Its potential presence was probably the reason for terminating joint ownership of the March line at Needingworth Junction which would have been a convenient point for the northern end of the curve. For many years Great Northern maps were drawn in such a way as to imply through running facilities from Huntington to March via St. Ives.

Goods traffic originating in the Ely and St. Ives area was almost entirely agricultural including an important seasonal component in fruit. From June to October, fruit was loaded at most stations in the area although the greatest tonnage was recorded at Wisbech, largely due to the inclusion in the returns of traffic originating on the Wisbech and Upwell Tramway. In 1922 the three busiest stations for fruit were:

	Tons goods	*Tons passenger*
Wisbech, including W and U Tramway	13,664	1,945
Long Stanton	2,823	305
Oakington	2,505	252

Loading took place mainly between 3.0 and 4.30 p.m. for early morning delivery to markets in London, Liverpool, Manchester, Leeds, Hull, etc. Northbound traffic was staged to Whitemoor and concentrated there into trains leaving at 7.0 p.m. for handling over to the Great Central at Pyewipe, and at 7.12 and 7.25 p.m. for Doncaster and beyond.

In the 1920s, sugar beet was developed as a crop in East Anglia. The resulting traffic was partly responsible for enlargement of the yards at Whitemoor. Locally in the area now covered, a large beet refinery was opened at Ely in 1924.

The through goods traffic passing Ely in the down direction may be considered as three main flows:

Trains from the Cambridge direction to the March, King's Lynn or Norwich lines.

Trains from the Fordham direction to March.

Trains using Ely West Curve in the down direction (towards March).

The regular down midweek goods trains in 1927 comprising these flows are summarised in *Tables 7* to *9*. The notes to the tables repeat any WTT notes which detail engine or crew workings. Truck trains (a Great Eastern term for empty wagon trains still used in the 1927 WTT) were augmented by 'when required' workings which were not, except in a few instances, detailed in the WTT. It is probable that a large proportion of the 'when required' workings from Temple Mills used the St. Ives route. The regular trains passing through St. Ives are listed in *Table 10*. It is noteworthy that the two down express goods trains, one to Whitemoor and one to Doncaster, were both routed via St. Ives in preference to

TABLE 7

ELY - GOODS TRAINS FROM THE CAMBRIDGE DIRECTION

Tuesdays to Fridays, Summer 1927

Class	*Train*	*To*		ELY *arr*	ELY *dep*
				a.m.	*a.m.*
A	9.40 p.m. Thames Wharf	March	Goods	1.45	2.3
A	11.40 p.m. Temple Mills	Norwich	Goods	pass 2.55	
C	8.7 p.m. Tottenham	Whitemoor	Goods	pass 3.55	
A	12.25 a.m. Tottenham	March	Goods	4.13	4.21
A	1.30 a.m. Tottenham	King's Lynn	Goods	4.36	5.10
A	4.40 a.m. Cambridge	March	Goods	5.15	5.45
B	1.50 a.m. Temple Mills	Norwich	Goods	5.55	6.10
C	2.5 a.m. Temple Mills	King's Lynn	Trucks	pass 5.36	
C	3.45 a.m. Temple Mills	Whitemoor	Goods	pass 7.21	
C	6.15 a.m. Temple Mills	Peterborough East	Goods	pass 9.41	
D	9.20 a.m. Cambridge	Wymondham	Stopping Goods	9.56	10.15
				p.m.	*p.m.*
C	12.10 p.m. Cambridge	Peterborough East	Goods	pass 12.50	
C	9.5 a.m. Temple Mills	Whitemoor	Goods	pass 1.30	
D	2.0 p.m. Cambridge	Littleport	Stopping Goods	2.45	3.0
C	12.40 p.m. Temple Mills	Peterborough East	Goods	pass 5.5	
C	1.20 p.m. Stratford	Whitemoor	Trucks	pass 5.55	

NOTES

8.7 p.m. ex-Tottenham: picked up at stations to Broxbourne, where first crew were relieved by men travelling as pasengers on 10.43 p.m. Liverpool Street.

9.40 p.m. ex-Thames Wharf: worked by March engine.

1.50 a.m. ex-Temple Mills: engine changed at Cambridge.

3.45 and 6.15 a.m. ex-Temple Mills: worked by Stratford engines.

Provision was made for 11 departures from Temple Mills to Peterborough East or Whitemoor of 'when required' Class C empty truck trains. Routeing via Ely or St. Ives was not specified

TABLE 8

ELY - GOODS TRAINS FROM THE FORDHAM DIRECTION

Tuesdays to Fridays, Summer 1927

Class	*Train*	*To*		ELY *arr*	ELY *dep*
				a.m.	*a.m.*
B	8.20 p.m. Ipswich	March	Goods	pass 12.0mn	
B	6.50 p.m. Chelmsford	March	Goods	pass 12.35	
B	11.30 p.m. Ipswich	March	Goods	3.10	3.35
C	4.10 a.m. Colchester	Peterborough East	Trucks	pass 9.10	
C	5.10 a.m. Parkeston	Whitemoor	Goods	pass 11.15	
				p.m.	*p.m.*
C	5.50 a.m. Colchester	March	Goods	pass 12.40	
C	10.15 a.m. Cambridge	Peterborough East	Goods	pass 1.15	
C	11.25 a.m. Ipswich	Peterborough East	Goods	pass 3.12	
B	11.55 a.m. Colchester	Peterborough East	Goods	3.45	3.50
A	11.40 a.m. Parkeston	Whitemoor	Goods	pass 5.40	
B	5.55 p.m. Bury	March	Goods	8.5	8.45
A	5.50 p.m. Ipswich	Peterborough East	Goods	pass 9.15	
C	7.15 p.m. Ipswich	Peterborough East	Goods	11.15	11.35

NOTES

10.15 a.m. ex-Cambridge: Ran via Newmarket. Cambridge men change en route with Peterborough East men (nominally at Newmarket).

5.55 p.m. ex-Bury: worked from Ely by March engine and men off 3.0 p.m. March.

Provision was made for 3 'when required' Class C trains from Ipswich to Peterborough East.

TABLE 9

ELY WEST CURVE - GOODS TRAINS IN THE DOWN DIRECTION (Towards March)

Tuesdays to Fridays, Summer 1927

Class	*Train*	*To*		ELY NORTH JCN *arr*	*dep*
				a.m.	*a.m.*
C	11.0 p.m. Norwich	Whitemoor	Goods	2.15	2.25
C	1.10 a.m. Yarmouth	Peterborough East	Trucks	pass 4.50	
C	5.30 a.m. Wensum Jcn.	Whitemoor	Goods	pass 10.10	
C	6.10 a.m. Norwich Victoria	Peterborough East	Trucks	pass 11.10	
				p.m.	*p.m.*
C	10.45 a.m. Lowestoft	Peterborough East	Trucks	pass 4.45	
A	2.15 p.m. Norwich	Whitemoor	Goods & Cattle	pass 5.45	
B	8.0 a.m. Norwich	March	Goods	pass 5.55	
A	3.50 p.m. (ThO) Yarmouth	Peterborough East	Goods	pass 8.40	
A	6.40 p.m. (ThX) Norwich	Whitemoor	Goods	9.50	10.0
A	7.20 p.m. (ThO) Norwich	Whitemoor	Goods	pass 10.55	
A	5.50 p.m. (ThX) Yarmouth	Peterborough East	Goods	pass 10.55	

NOTES

ThO Thursdays only

ThX Thursdays excepted

11.0 p.m. ex-Norwich: worked by Norwich engine

1.10 a.m. ex-Yarmouth: Peterborough East engine & men, out with the 6.30 a.m. Goods and Coal ex-Peterborough East on the previous day.

5.30 a.m. ex-Wensum Jcn: Norwich trainmen change with March where convenient.

6.10 a.m. ex-Norwich Victoria: Norwich trainmen change with Peterborough East at Brandon.

10.45 a.m. ex-Lowestoft: Peterborough East engine & men, out with 12.0 noon ex-Peterborough East on the previous day.

2.15 p.m. ex-Norwich: Norwich trainmen change with March at Shippea Hill.

3.50 p.m. ex-Yarmouth (ThO): Yarmouth engine & men, returning with 12.0 noon ex-Peterborough East on Fridays.

6.40 p.m. ex-Norwich (ThX): Norwich trainmen change with Peterborough East at Ely North Jcn.

Provision was made for 3 'when required' Class C trains from Norwich to Peterborough East via Ely West Curve

TABLE 10

ST. IVES - GOODS TRAINS FROM THE CAMBRIDGE DIRECTION

Tuesdays to Fridays, Summer 1927

Class	*Train*	*To*		ST. IVES *arr*	*dep*
				a.m.	*a.m.*
C	7.35 p.m. Park Yard	Peterborough East	Trucks	pass 12.37	
C	11.0 p.m. Goodmayes	Whitemoor	Trucks	pass 3.30	
C	1.15 a.m. Stratford Market	Whitemoor	Trucks	pass 5.2	
A	1.10 a.m. Thames Wharf	Whitemoor	Goods	5.27	5.37
A	5.30 a.m. Cambridge	March	Goods	6.5	6.45
C	3.50 a.m. Park Yard	Peterborough East	Trucks	pass 7.0	
D	6.25 a.m. Cambridge	March	Stopping Goods	9.20	10.25
				p.m.	*p.m.*
C	1.35 p.m. Cambridge	Warboys	Goods	2.20	2.55
LMS	1.42 p.m. Cambridge	Kettering	Goods	2.50	3.0
A	10.40 a.m. Temple Mills	Whitemoor	Goods	3.30	3.35
A	3.25 p.m. Cambridge	Whitemoor	Goods	5.18	5.33
LMS	4.20 p.m. Cambridge	Kettering	Goods	6.0	6.20
B	6.25 p.m. Cambridge	Peterborough East	Goods	7.10	7.25
LMS	7.45 p.m. Cambridge	Kettering	Goods	8.37	8.52
XpG2	6.20 p.m. Victoria Docks	Whitemoor	Goods	pass 10.2	
LMS	10.0 p.m. Cambridge	Kettering	Goods	pass 10.40	
XpG1	9.3 p.m. Spitalfields	Doncaster	Goods	pass 11.6	
A	5.0 p.m. Temple Mills	Whitemoor	Goods	pass 11.50	

NOTES

XpG1 No.1 Express Goods

XpG2 No.2 Express Goods

1.10 a.m. ex-Thames Wharf: worked by March engine.

6.20 p.m. ex-Victoria Docks: maximum load 40 wagons, 6 of which must be fully fitted and brake pipes connected to the engine.

9.3 p.m. ex-Spitalfields: load from Tottenham 40 wagons and brake.

See Note in Table 1 regarding 'when required' empty truck trains.

O4 No. 6227 with a down empty wagon train on the East Coast line at Dukeries Junction on 8th May 1946. H. C. CASSERLEY

Ely. The LMS despatched four goods trains each day from Cambridge to Kettering. West of Huntington these traversed a single line sparsely provided with loops and worked by the train staff and ticket system.

Some details of the engines and crew workings may be gleaned from the notes appended to the tables and also from the separate working notes for particular trains in the WTT which are too long to repeat except for selected examples given later.

Peterborough East worked a lodging turn to Lowestoft with the 1.30 p.m. Class C coal train. The return next day was made with the 10.45 a.m. Class C from Lowestoft. Yarmouth men lodged at Peterborough once a week after working the 3.50 p.m. Thursdays only Class A from Vauxhall, returning on Friday with the 12.0 noon Class C coal train. Apart from these lodging turns, most workings on the Ely to Norwich line involved the change-over of crews at an intermediate point. Peterborough East men changed over at Brandon with Yarmouth men on one and Norwich men on two Class C trains. Another Peterborough turn involved changing with Norwich men at Ely North Junction. March men changed with Norwich on two Class C trains, one at Thetford and the other at Shippea Hill. Norwich had a night turn at Ely at 11.0 p.m., engine and men returning with the 3.30 a.m. Class A. On the Cambridge line, workings were less defined but a typical method of manning down trains was for Stratford men to be relieved at Cambridge by March or Peterborough East crews, the Stratford men returning home 'on the cushions'.

Conditional paths or point-to-point running times were laid down for a large variety of 'when required' braked trains using the Joint Line north of March and passing through Ely North Junction. These included:

Horse boxes from Doncaster to Parkeston or Colchester via Ely Dock Junction and Ipswich.
Meat and Fish from Doncaster to Bishopsgate via Cambridge.
Fish from Doncaster to Norwich via Ely West Curve.
Fish from Yarmouth or Lowestoft to Doncaster via Ely West Curve.
Cattle from Norwich, Trowse, to Manchester via Ely West Curve and Lincoln (Engines to take water at Brandon and Spalding only).
Cattle ex Ireland from Birkenhead to Trowse via Doncaster and Ely West Curve.

Provision was also made for other 'when required' trains as follows:

Cattle from Temple Mills to Trowse.
Cattle from King's Lynn to Tufnell Park.
Vegetable traffic from the Ely area to King's Cross, worked to Ely by booked trains and combined into the 11.0 p.m. Class A 'when required', Ely to Peterborough North.

Although only indirectly connected with Ely and St. Ives, the existence of three return workings in each direction daily between Whitemoor and Annesley is worth noting. These trains were worked by Great Eastern section locomotives and crews. From Annesley to Whitemoor with loaded coal, 35 wagons could be taken by No. 3 class engines (J15) and 45 by No. 4 class (J16 or J17), No. 5 class (J18 or J19) and No. 6 class (J20) engines. The workings were:

O2 No. 63959 with a Whitemoor to Temple Mills coal train near Broxbourne on 23rd June 1949. D. A. DANT

(1) Light engine from Annesley. Loaded from Mansfield Colliery Sidings dep. 2.15 a.m., via Clipstone Junction, the LDECR, Pyewipe Junction and the Joint line to Whitemoor, arr. 7.50 a.m.
(2) Annesley Sidings dep. 9.15 a.m. via Duckmanton South Junction, the LDECR, thence as for (1) to Whitemoor arr. 5.0 p.m.
(3) Annesley, Engine and Brake dep. 8.10 p.m., loaded from New Hucknall Sidings dep. 9.10 p.m., route as for (2), Whitemoor, arr. 5.13 a.m.

Two daily through trains also ran to Whitemoor from Markham Junction with coal from Bolsover, Markham and Grassmoor Collieries, attaching coal at Warsop Junction from Warsop, Shirebrook and Sherwood Collieries. The engines for these workings were serviced at Staveley. The use of Great Eastern section engines on the Annesley and Markham Junction workings was doubtless a legacy from the early days of the Lancashire, Derbyshire and East Coast Railway. The Great Eastern possessed a financial interest in the enterprise and was recompensated by running powers over the complete LDECR system, including a non-exercised access to Sheffield over the Sheffield District railway.

Before a glance at the branch line workings it is worth repeating some of the more interesting of the detailed working notes for goods trains.

1.30 a.m. Tottenham to King's Lynn.
'To work from Tottenham all traffic for Ely, King's Lynn line, March Wisbech and via Whitemoor. Load to be made up at Tottenham with Common User Wagons of 11.22 and 11.50 p.m. Local ex Spitalfields, which are to be placed among the King's Lynn traffic (unmarshalled). London goods for St. Ives off 11.50 p.m. ex Spitalfields are to be attached to this train at Tottenham, next to March and Wisbech traffic.

Formation: Engine – Ely section, March and Wisbech traffic, Waterbeach, Lakenheath and Harling Road to Attleboro' road wagons – King's Lynn section unmarshalled – Brake.

To work King's Lynn and M&GN tranship wagons. To take water at Bishops Stortford and work King's Lynn mailbags from that station. To detach at Whittlesford wagons with London sheds goods for March and Wisbech and St. Ives to go forward on 1.10 a.m. ex Thames Wharf and goods for Waterbeach, Lakenheath and Harling Road to Attleboro' to go forward on 1.50 a.m. ex Temple Mills.'

1.45 a.m. Whitemoor to Temple Mills.
'Wagons containing Loco Coal for Chingford are to be attached as follows:

Monday and Tuesday – 4 wagons each day.
Wednesday to Saturday (inclusive) 5 wagons each day.

These wagons to be detached at Park Yard and sent foward by 1.0 p.m. to Hoe Street and attached there to 12.45 a.m. Temple Mills to Chingford. The 1.45 a.m. to be worked by March power on Saturdays, trainmen to return after rest at Stratford.'

5.25 p.m. Peteroborough East to Brentwood.
'Conveys goods and coal traffic for Brentford and district viz: Brentwood, Brooklands, Brooklands Siding, Chelmsford, Church's Siding, Cold Norton, Hatfield Peverel, Heath's Sidings, Ingatestone, Inworth, Kelvedon, Maldon East, Maldon West, Mark's Tey, Mountnessing Siding, Old Hall Siding, Shenfield, Tiptree, Tolleshunt, Tolleshunt D'Arcy, Tollesbury, Tudwick Road Siding, Wickham Bishops, Witham.

Trainmen to be relieved at Colchester and return with 11.55 a.m. (Mons and Sats excepted), 12.10 p.m. (Sats only) Colchester to Peterborough East following day. Engine to be turned at Shenfield. Engine to be used to work empty coal wagons Brentwood to Shenfield and afterwards work 3.25 a.m. Shenfield to Marks Tey'.

Finally a general note:

'When signals are lowered for up goods and coal trains to run through Bishops Stortford, engine drivers should check the speed to about 20 miles per hour when passing the station to enable the guard to throw out the Control advice note'.

The branch from St. Ives to Huntington had a chequered early history, an overworked phrase, but

J19/2 No. 8144 near St. Ives about 1945. AUTHOR'S COLLECTION

J39 No. 64776 with an up Class B goods train at Audley End on 26th August 1953. L. R. PETERS

really justified in this instance. It was originally intended to form part of the Ely to Bedford Railway to link the Lynn and Ely with the Bedford branch of the London and Birmingham. Cut back to Huntington by the 1845 Parliament, it became a pawn in railway politics, the Ely to St. Ives portion remaining unbuilt. Until the Midland completed the line from Kettering to Huntington in 1866, traffic was negligible and at one stage it was worked by a horse tram. It was also used for wagon storage thus anticipating the fate of many branch lines by some 100 years. St. Ives and Ely were finally linked via Sutton in 1878.

The LMS trains between St. Ives and Huntingdon are included in *Table 10*. In the 1930s, A Hitchin LNER engine and men made a round trip which traversed this section on Mondays to Fridays. The first leg was all stations to Huntingdon with the 7.22 p.m. passenger from Hitchin, arriving at 8.15 p.m. From Huntingdon the 9.25 p.m. Class A goods to Cambridge was worked. The Cambridge arrival was at 10.45 p.m. They were back home at Hitchin at 1.45 a.m. having worked direct from Cambridge with the 12.30 a.m. Class A goods. In 1927, Great Northern section workings from Huntington were limited to one 'suspended' and two 'when required' goods trains. These left Huntingdon East at 5.30 a.m. (suspended) and (when required) at 8.10 a.m. and 9.9 p.m. The 8.10 a.m. returned as engine and brake, the other two turns were classified as goods in both directions.

The branch from Somersham to Ramsey had a return goods turn marked in the WTT as 'suspended' which was timed to be worked by the Ramsay East engine before its first passenger working of the day. (5.50 a.m. goods ex-Ramsey East arriving back at 7.20 a.m. to work the 7.36 a.m. passenger). The suspension of this turn left Ramsey East without a goods train except on Saturdays when a trip was made between the morning and afternoon passenger trains. The 3.5 p.m. ex Ramsey and the 6.10 p.m. ex Somersham passenger trains were, however, classed as mixed, the former 'to clear Ramsey E of important traffic. Not to attach at Warboys' and the latter 'May work cattle from Somersham to Ramsay East. Somersham to work brake goods to Warboys and Ramsey East by goods trains only.' Warboys, with its brickworks, had the distinction of being the terminating point at 3.35 p.m. of the 1.35 p.m. goods from Cambridge. The return working left Warboys at 4.15 p.m. and ran through to Park Yard, Tottenham; 'Trainmen to be relieved at Cambridge on arrival. Engine to run light Park Yard to Temple Mills, on goods line to Tottenham thence on Main Line and, after being turned at Temple Mills, to work special as required.'

The Ely to St. Ives branch generated little traffic and lost its passenger service as early as 1931. In 1927 a daily stopping goods, worked by Ely enginemen and guard, left Ely at 10.20 a.m., arriving at St. Ives at 1.10 p.m. The return working did not leave St. Ives until 6.45 p.m.

When this picture was taken of a short local goods train near Newmarket, J17 No. 8155, running tender-first, was not carrying a headlamp code. S. H. FREESE

(except on Saturdays); presumably the afternoon was occupied by shunting. On Mondays only a goods ran from Ely at 7.5 a.m., arriving at St. Ives at 8.20 a.m.; 'A carriage to be attached for use of drovers, to work Cattle from Stations between Ely and St. Ives.'

The motive power requirements for working goods traffic on the Great Eastern were more onerous than might appear at first sight. A Martian landing in the Ely district would be forgiven for reporting that the Earth is actually two-dimensional. There are, however, some significant gradients on the Ely to Norwich line, on which J20s were not permitted in 1927. From Brandon the climb off the fens includes 2¼ miles at 1 in 267 between Two Mile Bottom box and Thetford and 1½ miles at 1 in 200 before Roudham Junction. In the up direction there are 3 miles at 1 in 129 steepening to 1 in 101 through Hethersett. On the Cambridge main lines, Elsenham is the summit of long gradual climbs in each direction. Loaded coal had to be worked against the collar nearly all the way from Shelford, some 17 miles with a sharp downhill break after Audley End. The worst pitch is 1½ miles at 1 in 176 before Elsenham. Northbound there is a gradual rise from the Lea at Copper Mill Junction for some 30 miles to Elsenham, the otherwise easy gradients concluding with 1½ miles at 1 in 124 to 1 in 107.

The GER goods tender locomotive stock handed over to the LNER at grouping consisted of relatively few classes of 0-6-0s. Commendably all had some element of standardisation with the passenger engines. The classes are summarised in *Table 11* which highlight a perennial difficulty on the GER, that of brakes. As a Westinghouse line surrounded by vacuum neighbours (GNR, GCR, LNWR and Midland) the GER was celebrated for the foreign workings that its passenger and mixed traffic locomotives undertook with specials and excursions using Westinghouse fitted stock. It was necessary to provide some goods engines with the Westinghouse brake for branch duties involving both passenger and goods workings; some engines with vacuum ejectors, including *Claud Hamilton*, were also required for fitted goods trains. Apart from the remaining N31s (LNER J14), Westinghouse brakes on goods engines were confined to J15s, the most versatile class for branch working. The large engines of classes J19 and J20 had vacuum ejectors. They could not, however, work passenger trains on their home ground until the eventual conversion of passenger stock to vacuum. Intermediately, classes J16, J17 and J18 were purely goods and mineral engines, but all those built as J18s eventually received vacuum ejectors in the course of rebuilding. Comparatively late in their lives, outside the scope of *Table 11*, some J17s were also fitted with vacuum ejectors.

The stringent limits of weight and length imposed on the design of express locomotives for the Great Eastern section are well known. Greater freedom was allowed for goods locomotives and the final GER design, LNER class J20 used the boiler, cylinders and motion of the B12 on the six-wheeled chassis. The result was an engine with a greater tractive capability than any other 0-6-0 in Great Britain until the advent of the Bulleid Q1s on the Southern Railway. A comparison of B12 and J20 weights shows the additional axle loading which was permitted for a goods locomotive compared with the ultimate GER passenger design.

TABLE 11
GER GOODS LOCOMOTIVES TAKEN INTO LNER STOCK

LNER Class	*GER Class*	*Designer*	*No. of Engines 1/1/23*	*Built*	*Withdrawn*	*Southern Area Load Class*	*BRAKE SYSTEM* *Steam*	*Steam & Vacuum Ejector*	*W'house*	*W'house & Vacuum Ejector*	*Remarks*
J14	N31	J. Holden	18	1893-1898	1908-1925	-	13	-	3	2	As J15, but with valves below cylinders. Cylinders standard with T19
J15	Y14	T.W. Worsdell	272	1883-1913	1922-1962	3	232	-	5	35	Valves between cylinders. Boilers on later engines standard with E4, F3 and J14
J16	F48	J. Holden	46	1900-1903	Rebuilt to J17 by 1932	4	46	-	-	-	Boilers and cylinders standard with D14 (round topped firebox, non-superheated)
J17	G58	J. Holden	44	1902-1911	1954-1956	4	44	-	-	-	Boilers and cylinders standard with D15 (Belpaire firebox, superheated 1915-32)
J18	E72	A.J. Hill	10	1912-1913	Rebuilt to J19 by 1936	5	10	-	-	-	Boilers standard with D15, cylinders and valves standard with B12. Vacuum Ejectors fitted when rebuilt to J19/2
J19	T77	A.J. Hill	25	1916-1920	1958-1962	5	-	25	-	-	As J18, but without tail rods. Rebuilt with round topped fireboxes as J19/2, 1934-39
J20	D81	A.J. Hill	25	1920-1922	1959-1962	6	-	25	-	-	Boiler, cylinders and motion standard with B12. Rebuilt with round topped fireboxes as J20/1, 1943-56

J20 No. 8275 with an up coal train at Trumpington in 1935.
LOCOMOTIVE PUBLISHING CO.

J19 No. 8262 at Stratford on 9th August 1934. In 1935 it was rebuilt with a round-topped firebox and classified J19/2.
G. T. STAMP

J18 No. 8244. Originally fitted with a steam brake only, a vacuum ejector was added when it was rebuilt as Class J 19/2 in 1935.
PHOTOMATIC

O4 No. 6313 with a train of empty wagons bound for Whitemoor passing Trumpington box in 1932.

LOCOMOTIVE PUBLISHING CO.

	B12 tons cwt	*J20* tons cwt
Total Engine Weight	63 0	54 15
Maximum Axle Load	15 13	18 16

The J20s were always associated with the coal traffic on the Cambridge main line. No. 8280 was experimentally fitted with Lentz poppet valves in 1925 and trials, using the dynamometer car, were held between Stratford and Whitemoor, No 8280 being compared with No. 8287 which retained the standard piston valves.

Soon after the formation of the LNER, some K2 2-6-0s were drafted to the Great Eastern section. In view of the limits applied to express engines, it is probable that they were passed by the Civil Engineer for goods traffic only. They were, however, to be found on passenger trains at times, as also was the case with the later arrivals of class J39. The sight – and sound – of a K2 on an up Southend fast passing over the South Street bridge at Romford at what seemed nearer to 70 than 60 mph is not easily forgotten.

From 1929, O4s supplemented the J20s on the Whitemoor to Temple Mills coal trains. Three years later, the first of the new series of O2s was allocated to March for working these trains. Eventually it was joined by 15 others. The permitted numbers of loaded wagons in the up direction were 55 for a J20, 60 for an O4 and 65 for an O2. Wartime brought the USA 2-8-0s to the GE section and the generations of steam locomotives were brought to a close with the O7 ex-WD 2-8-0s. In contrast to the position with express passenger traffic, there were few restrictions on the employment of suitable goods locomotives on the ex-GER.

There is a great contrast in the changes wrought by the passing years to the railways of St. Ives and Ely. The Ely to St. Ives branch was severed at Earith Bridge in 1958 and thereafter was worked as two separate sections. This was the commencement of successive closures which eventually left March as a wayside station between Ely and Peterborough. Ely, however, has only suffered the loss of the branch to St. Ives and there must be only a few provincial centres which have retained such a large proportion of their original configuration. It is still a focal point of traffic, but now of passengers rather than goods, having become an important junction on the Sprinter route from the Midlands and the North West to East Anglia. The Joint line itself has been closed between March and Spalding and this has resulted in the saddest change of all, the complete closure of the yards at Whitemoor, once the pride of the LNER.

Sources:
LNER, Great Eastern Section Working Time Table, Summer 1927.
Railway Magazine: April 1910, March 1915, Sept 1923, June 1924.
A Regional History of the Railways of Great Britain, Vol. 5, The Eastern Counties, D. I. Gordon (David and Charles, 1968)

Austerity 2–8–0 running as LNER Class O7 No. 3013 with a down Class B goods at Cambridge in 1947. L. R. PETERS

Class O2/3 built at Doncaster in 1932 and allocated from new to March to work coal trains from Whitemoor to Temple Mills. REAL PHOTOGRAPHS

Colwick shed yard in 1928 with No. 3131 at the head of a line of R1 class locomotives and on the right J6 No. 3573 standing in front of a K1. L&GRP

CHAPTER FIVE

THE NOTTINGHAM TO GRANTHAM LINE IN 1935

O4 No. 6327 heading an up coal train on the four-track section between Radcliffe and Saxondale Junction. H. GORDON TIDEY

THE major part of the LNER Nottingham to Grantham line was built by the Ambergate Nottingham Boston and Eastern Junction Railway ('The Ambergate'). The actual construction achieved by this rather grandly titled enterprise extended from the Midland Railway at Carlton Junction, some three miles east of Nottingham, to the canal basin at Grantham. In 1851 the Ambergate was offered a working agreement by the LNWR and Midland jointly. This was accepted by the directors but rejected by the shareholders due to the voting power of Graham Hutchison of Glasgow who had purchased a large holding. Mr Hutchison had been a director of the Great Northern Railway since February 1850. Negotiations followed which resulted in an agreement for the GNR to work the line from 1st July 1852. The terms of the agreement gave rise to legal wrangles culminating in the celebrated imprisonment by the Midland of the first Great Northern locomotive to reach Nottingham. The dispute with the Midland was settled in May 1853 by a pooling agreement for competitive traffic. In 1860 the Ambergate acknowledged the renouncement of its early ambitions by changing its name to the Nottingham and Grantham Railway and Canal Co. It was leased by the GNR from 1st August 1861, remaining an independent concern until Grouping in 1923. For practical operating purposes it was, however, part of the GNR. A reminder of its original title was maintained into recent times by the Ambergate Yard at Grantham.

In some instances the Great Northern was forced into unsatisfactory agreements in the process of protecting its interests from competition, but gaining control of the 19 miles from Colwick to Grantham, due to Mr Hutchison's 'cornering' of Ambergate shares, was an exceptionally fortunate event. The result was access not only to Nottingham itself but also, more importantly, to Nottinghamshire coalfield which provided the GNR and later the LNER with a heavy and remunerative mineral traffic through the years.

The growth of the mineral traffic is well illustrated by the scale of the enlargements made to the yards at Colwick where the coal was concentrated. In the 24 years from 1876 to 1900 the siding capacity was increased from 1,150 to 6,000 wagons. The first engine shed, opened in 1876, was already needing extension in 1882, by which time 50 locomotives were housed. In 1896 another shed was required and by 1912 the Colwick motive power district was second only to London in size, with some 250 locomotives including those at Derby and Pinxton.

The Nottingham to Grantham line was without dramatic features. Although the gradients included some comparatively steep pitches, these were short enough to permit train loadings similar to those on the main line. The route eastward from Nottingham as finally developed is shown diagrammatically in *Fig. 6*.

At Bottesford the connection to the Newark line gave access to Doncaster. A connecting link from Allington Junction to Barkston East Junction led to Sleaford and

Table 12
NOTTINGHAM TO GRANTHAM GOODS TRAFFIC
DAILY ENGINE AND CREW WORKINGS SPECIFIED IN WTT, SUMMER 1935

Loco class	*Load wagons*	*Train class*	*Details* *Dep.*		*Arr.*	
				BOSTON SHED		
3	-	A Goods	Boston	7.15 p.m.	Colwick	9.35 p.m.
		B Goods	Colwick	12.05 a.m.	Boston	3.00 a.m.
3	-	A Goods	Boston	8.40 p.m.	Colwick	11.09 p.m.
	-	B Goods	Colwick	1.15 a.m.	Boston	4.24 a.m.
3	-	A Goods	Boston	10.50 p.m.	Colwick	2.04 a.m.
	-	B Goods	Colwick	4.25 a.m.	Boston	8.18 a.m.
				COLWICK SHED		
7	70	C Mineral	Colwick	2.30 a.m.	New England	5.42 a.m.
	-	A Empties	New England	6.45 a.m.	Colwick	9.01 a.m.
7	65	C Mineral	Nott'm Goods	4.05 a.m.	New England	7.25 a.m.
	-	A Empties	New England	9.00 a.m.	Colwick	11.32 a.m.
3	-	A Empties	Colwick	6.45 a.m.	Denton	8.20 a.m.
	-	C Mineral	Denton	11.10 a.m.	Colwick	12.36 a.m.
3	-	A Goods	Colwick	9.55 a.m.	Denton	12.50 p.m.
	-		Denton	4.55 p.m.	Colwick	6.15 p.m.
7 (Note 1)	70	B Empties	Colwick	12.30 p.m.	Highdyke	2.48 p.m.
	-	C Mineral	Highdyke	4.20 p.m.	Colwick	5.48 p.m.
3	-	B Goods	Colwick	1.38 p.m.	Sleaford	5.09 p.m.
	-	A Goods	Sleaford	7.32 p.m.	Colwick	9.22 p.m.
7	65	C Mineral	Nott'm Goods	4.20 p.m.	New England	8.10 p.m.
	-	B Goods	New England	9.55 p.m.	Colwick	1.23 a.m.
7	-	C Mineral	Colwick	5.15 p.m.	New England	8.20 p.m.
	-	A Empties	New England	10.45 p.m.	Colwick	1.32 a.m.
K2	-	No. 2 Braked	Colwick	8.55 p.m.	New England	10.58 p.m.
	-	A Empties	New England	1.00 a.m.	Colwick	3.56 a.m.
B8 (Note 2)	-	No. 2 Braked	Colwick	9.45 p.m.	Hull	2.02 a.m.
	-	No. 1 Braked	Hull	8.20 p.m.	Colwick	10.45 p.m.
K2 (Lodging)	-	No. 2 Braked	Colwick	11.00 p.m.	Hull	4.35 p.m.
	-	No. 2 Braked	Hull	10.55 p.m.	Nott'm Goods	5.10 a.m.
				DONCASTER SHED		
K2	-	No. 2 Braked	Decoy	6.10 a.m.	Colwick	9.28 a.m.
	-	B Goods	Colwick	11.30 a.m.	Decoy	5.20 p.m.
2 (Note 3)	-	B Goods	Decoy	12.20 p.m.	Colwick	6.01 p.m.
	-	B Empties	Colwick	6.50 p.m.	Doncaster Mineral	10.15 p.m.
				GRANTHAM SHED		
7 (Note 4)	-	B Mineral	Highdyke	8.55 p.m.	Colwick	10.28 p.m.
	-	B Empties	Colwick	11.55 p.m.	Highdyke	2.15 a.m.
				NEW ENGLAND SHED		
K3 (Note 5)	60	No. 1 Braked	Westwood	12.12 a.m.	Colwick	1.45 a.m.
	-	C Mineral	Colwick	3.05 a.m.	New England	7.05 a.m.
K2	-	A Empties	New England	12.30 a.m.	Colwick	3.02 a.m.
	-	C Mineral	Colwick	7.00 a.m.	New England	10.45 a.m.
K3 (Note 6)	-	No. 2 Braked	New England	2.20 a.m.	Nott'm Goods	4.40 a.m.
	-	C Mineral	Colwick	6.15 a.m.	New England	10.20 a.m.
7	-	B Goods	Westwood	9.55 a.m.	Colwick	1.02 p.m.
	-	C Mineral	Colwick	2.30 p.m.	New England	6.10 p.m.
8	-	C Empties	New England	3.45 p.m.	Colwick	6.30 p.m.
	80	C Mineral	Colwick	7.55 p.m.	New England	11.55 p.m.
K3 (Note 7)	-	No. 2 Braked	Westwood	8.20 p.m.	Colwick	9.55 p.m.
	-	No. 1 Braked	Colwick	12.40 a.m.	New England	2.04 a.m.
K3	60	No. 1 Braked	New England	11.30 p.m.	Colwick	12.44 a.m.
	55	No. 2 Braked	Colwick	3.45 a.m.	New England	5.19 a.m.
				YORK/COLWICK SHEDS (Alternate Nights)		
J39	-	B Goods	York, Dringhouses	11.20 p.m.	Colwick	7.11 a.m.
	-	B Goods	Colwick	12.45 a.m.	York	7.05 a.m.

NOTES

1. The engine commenced the return journey from Highdyke tender first. 15 minutes were allowed at Grantham for turning.
2. 7.45 p.m. Burton to Hull, Hessle Junction, returning with the 8.20 p.m. Hull to Burton. A lodging turn, Colwick engine and Derby men, shared with a Dairycoates B16 and men on alternate nights. The Dairycoates men lodged at Derby.
3. This working is given as specified in the WTT although it involved a very long day with only a nominal 49 minutes at Colwick. The use of a Load 2 engine is also doubted.
4. The length of the 11.55 p.m. from Colwick was limited to 40 ten-ton wagons.
5. The outward train was the 9.00 p.m. from King's Cross to Huskisson.
6. The outward train was the 10.00 p.m. King's Cross to Nottingham.
7. The outward train was the 3.10 p.m. King's Cross to Deansgate.
8. The outward train was the 8.30 p.m. King's Cross to Deansgate. The return train continued to London, East Goods, arriving at 10.15 a.m.

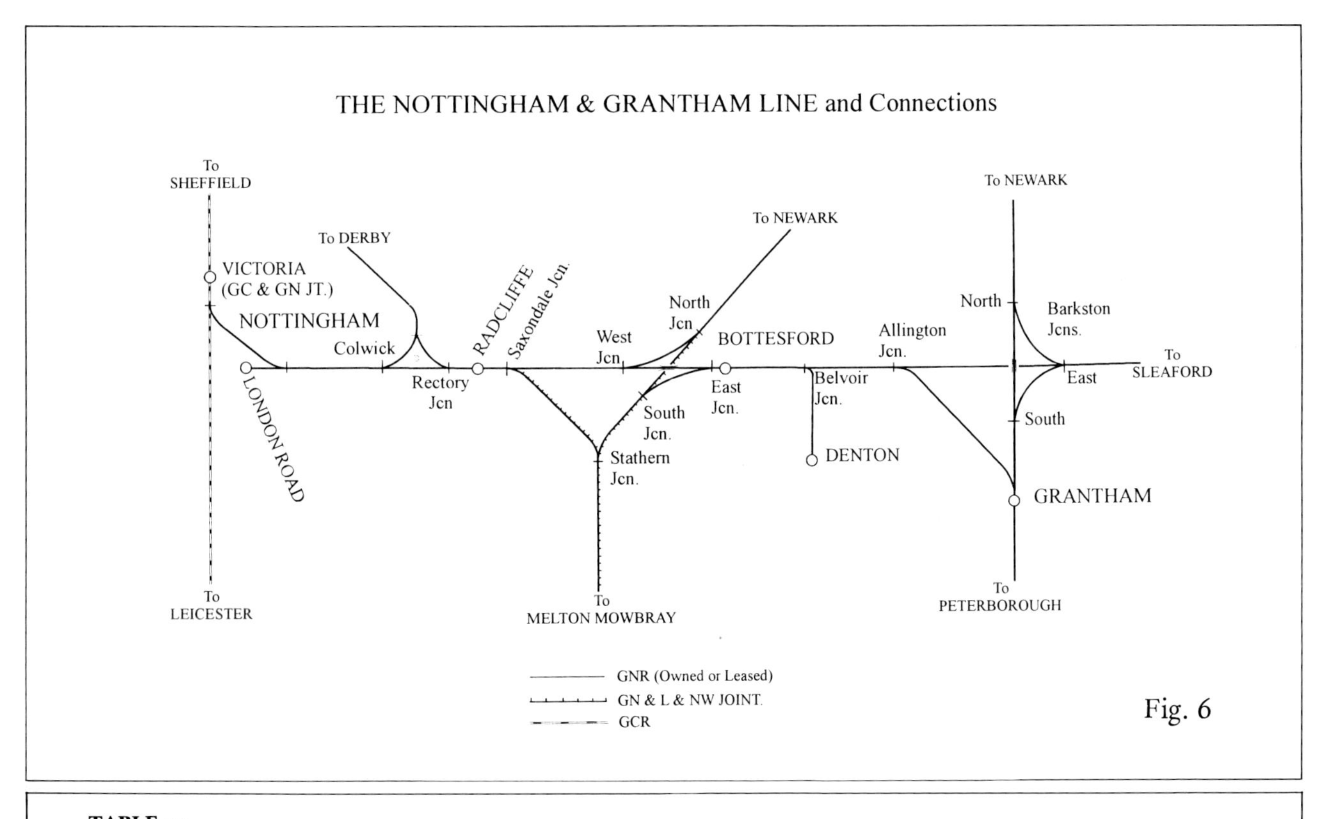

Fig. 6

TABLE 13

NOTTINGHAM TO GRANTHAM GOODS TRAFFIC
DAILY GOODS TRAINS WITH INCOMPLETE DETAILS OF WORKINGS, SUMMER 1935

Loco class	*Train class*	*From*	*To*	*No. of trains*	*Notes*
-	A Goods	Colwick	New England	1	
7	B Goods	Colwick	New England	1	
7	C Mineral	Colwick	New England	3	
-	D Pick-up	Colwick	Grantham	1	
7	B Goods	Colwick	Whitemoor	2	
7	C Mineral	Colwick	Whitemoor	5	
3	B Goods	Colwick	York	1	
K3	No. 1 Braked	Colwick	New England	1	1
-	B Goods	Colwick	Doncaster	1	2
-	B Goods	Doncaster	Colwick	1	2
-	B Goods	Doncaster	Colwick	1	3
-	B Good	Colwick	Grantham	1	4
-	D Pick-up	Grantham	Colwick	1	4
-	B Good	Grantham	Colwick	2	
3	A Goods	York, Dringhouses	Colwick	1	
2	B Goods	Hull	Colwick	1	5
-	B Empties	New England	Colwick	1	
7	A Goods	Whitemoor	Nott'm Goods	1	
7	A Empties	Whitemoor	Colwick	1	
7	B Empties	Whitemoor	Colwick	2	
7	C Empties	Whitemoor	Colwick	3	

1. 4.55 p.m. Huskisson to London, East Goods, 1.50 a.m. ex Colwick.
2. Colwick engine, 1.55 a.m. ex Colwick, 5.50 p.m. ex Doncaster Decoy, no crew details.
3. 6.10 a.m. ex Doncaster Decoy. Per WTT the trainmen changed at Retford but there are records of Doncaster men working through to Colwick on this train.
4. Colwick engine, 4.45 a.m. ex Colwick, 8.30 a.m. ex Grantham, Colwick arr. 4.28 p.m. No crew details.
5. 3.55 a.m. ex Hull, 6.17 a.m. ex Decoy with Doncaster engine and men, 'engine to return with special to Doncaster as required'.

GNR Class Q1 No. 409 with an up coal train at Radcliffe in 1922. L&GRP

The GNR 0–6–0s took their turn on coal trains from Colwick. This view shows J22 (LNER J5) No. 28 taking a heavy load through Radcliffe. L&GRP

Colwick found employment for mixed traffic classes on mineral workings. This view shows K1 No. 1633 with an up coal train at Radcliffe in 1922. L&GRP

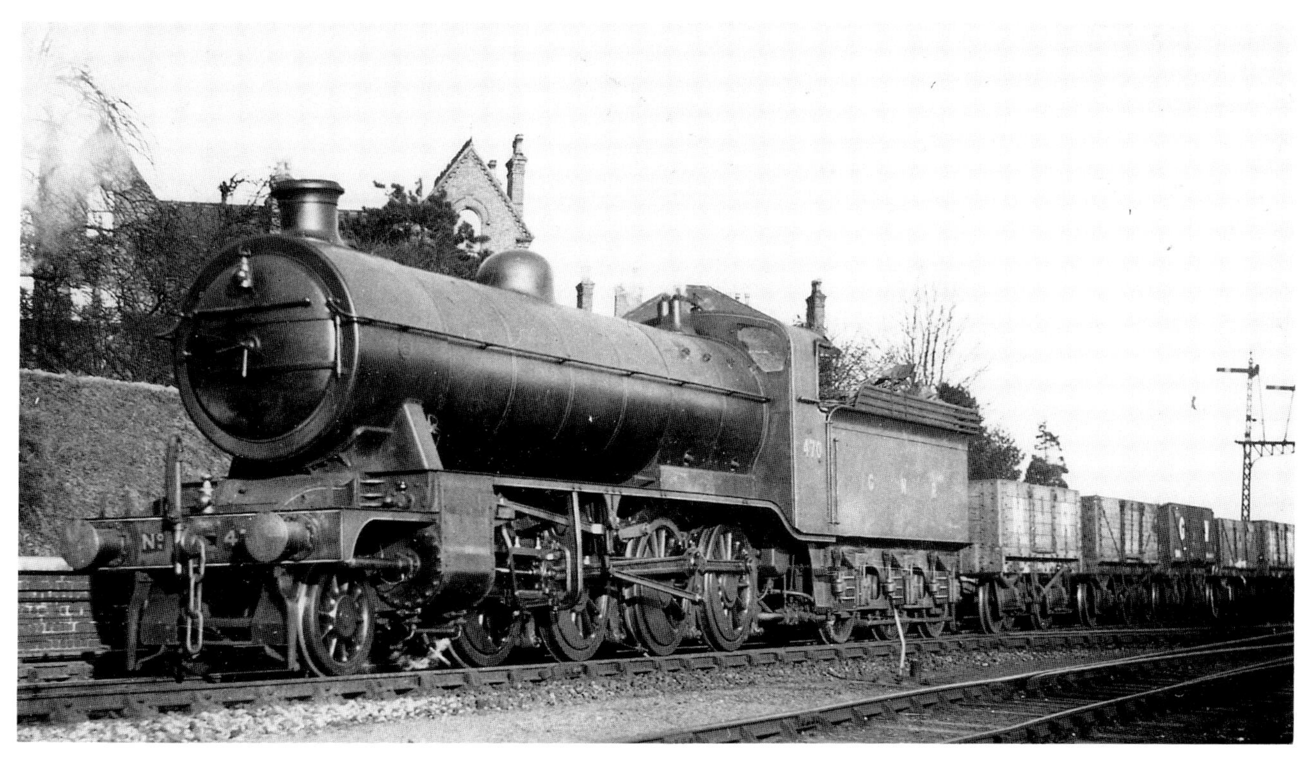

O1 No. 470 nearing the end of its journey to Colwick with a Class B goods at Radcliffe in 1922. L&GRP

East Lincolnshire and also, via the GN and GE Joint line, provided a valuable route to Whitemoor. This link was sufficiently busy in Great Northern days for Marston box to be established as an intermediate block post, open for two shifts, some two miles east of Allington Junction. Marston had, however, been closed by the 1930s. Additional up and down goods lines from Radcliffe to Saxondale Junction were opened in 1890 and on the approach to Grantham an up loop was provided between Gonerby and Barrowby Road boxes.

Midweek in the summer of 1935, the Saxondale Junction to Bottesford West Junction section was used by 86 booked goods and mineral trains daily. There was some imbalance between up and down trains but in total, east of Allington Junction, 42 trains used the Grantham line and 22 the Sleaford line. Eighteen trains traversed the curve between Bottesford West and North Junctions, leaving the total to be made up by two workings in each direction for the iron ore traffic from Denton via Belvoir Junction. Some iron ore originated also on the branch line from Highdyke south of Grantham, but by far the greater proportion of the mineral traffic was coal travelling east.

The working timetable makes no mention of conditional trains so the numbers given above must be taken as typical. The Nottingham district WTT, however, contained an unusually large amount of information concerning engine and crew workings and it is possible to detail much of the traffic in such terms. *Table 12* is a list of all workings for which complete details are known. Trains which are not included in *Table 12* are summarised in *Table 13*. In most instances the LNER Southern Area Loading Classification was quoted rather than a particular class of locomotive. For convenience the details of the relevant classes covered by the classifications are given below:

Load Class 2	J1, J2, J3, J4
Load Class 3	J5, J6, J11
Load Class 5	B8, J39, K2
Load Class 7	O4
Load Class 8	O1, O2

The preponderance of Class 7 engines on mineral trains was due to the availability of large numbers of ex-ROD O4s. These replaced a variety of Great Northern types. A series of photographs taken at Radcliffe in 1921 and 1922 includes coal or empty wagon trains hauled by the following classes: 0-6-0 – J5, J6; 0-8-0 – Q1, Q2; 2-6-0 – K1, K2; 2-8-0 – O1. (The more familiar LNER classifications are used.)

Curiously the only photograph of the R1 0-8-2T in the series is of No. 123, a non-superheated engine, running light although contemporary writers recorded the use of superheated R1s on Colwick to New England coal trains. It is probable that engines with a load classification superior to that allocated in the WTT were sometimes used. For instance it is difficult to envisage through working to Doncaster being limited to engines no larger than J3s. Class 8 engines were mentioned only once, for a train loading to 80 wagons, but O1s and O2s would possibly have been used indiscriminately with O4s by

J3 No. 3351 with a long coal train near Werrington in 1925. L&GRP

New England for their Class 7 duties. The class of engine for the 12.20 a.m. Colwick to Peterborough was given as 'A'. To the end of their days the J6s continued to be known as 'A engines' but officially this Great Northern classification was superseded in 1924; nevertheless it still appeared in the WTT eleven years later.

Journey times for the 47 miles from Colwick to New England were convenient for out and home turns within the eight-hour day. From Colwick to Whitemoor was 69 miles and the longer running times precluded the completion of the double journey in one shift. Stops for 'locomotive purposes' were booked at Sleaford, i.e. longer than a water stop, and it is possible that changeovers between Colwick and March crews were arranged there. The alternative would have been lodging turns, but definite information on this point is lacking.

A working which defied tabulation was the 5.5 a.m. Class B Goods from Colwick to Newark. This train was assigned to a Colwick D2. After arrival at Newark at 6.5 a.m. the 7.5 a.m. passenger was worked to Grantham. In the afternoon the remanned engine worked through to Stafford but the first set of men returned to Colwick with the King's Cross Milk Empties at 10.40 from Grantham.

Some trains had interesting continuations west of Colwick. The 11.10 a.m. Mineral from Denton exchanged its J6 for an O4 which took the load of ironstone to the Stanton Ironworks via Ilkeston. The 3.10 p.m. No. 2 Braked Goods from King's Cross to Manchester (Deansgate) picked up vegetable traffic at Biggleswade, Sandy and (when required) Tempsford. From Colwick the Leen Valley extension was used to Langwith Junction, thence the route was via the ex-LD&ECR to Sheffield and over Woodhead. The same route was followed by the 9.0 p.m. King's Cross to Huskisson on which a Peterborough guard worked through from Westwood to Heaton Mersey.

The other through working from King's Cross to Deansgate, the 8.30 p.m. No. 1 Braked Goods, took a different route. Although straying somewhat from the strict subject matter covered by the title of this chapter, it is worth recording the details of the Colwick to Deansgate portion of its journey. From 1895 the GNR held running powers over both the Peak Forest and Totley routes to Manchester of the Midland Railway and these, at least via Totley, continued to be exercised by the LNER. The LMS was reached via a short (55 chains) link, owned by the LNER, from the Pinxton branch at Brinsley Junction to Codnor Park Great Northern Junction on the ex-MR Erewash Valley line. The 8.30 p.m. left Colwick at 1.15 a.m. and passed Codnor Park at 2.25 a.m. The route thence to Manchester was via Chesterfield, Dore South and West Junction, Hathersage (stop for water), Chinley and New Mills South Junction (pass 4.2 a.m.) with an arrival at Deansgate at 5.0 a.m. The load from Colwick was limited to 37 fully fitted wagons and a brake van. The return working over the same route was the 8.22 p.m. Class A goods which also stopped for water at Hathersage and reached Colwick at 12.29 a.m. Fitted traffic for London went forward on the 4.55 p.m. from Huskisson at 1.50 a.m., advantage being taken of the increased loadings permitted south of Colwick. Between Deansgate and Colwick both up and down trains were worked by a single Trafford Park crew, a shift of at least nine hours even if the down train ran to time. In 1935 the locomotives were alternately J6s from Colwick and J11s or J39s from Trafford Park.

The LMS laid down detailed instructions for the procedure to be followed of an LNER locomotive failed on their territory;

FAILURE OF ENGINES WORKING L.N.E. FREIGHT TRAINS BETWEEN MANCHESTER AND CODNOR PARK

Between New Mills and Codnor Park.

In the event of failure of an engine working an L.N.E. freight train over the L.M.S. Railway between New Mills and Codnor Park the L.M.S. Company will provide an engine to work up trains forward to Brinsley Junction and down trains forward to Manchester (Deansgate), and the control offices must be advised to make the arrangements as shown below:

Gowhole Control Office between New Mills and Hathersage exclusive;

Masboro' Control Office between Hathersage and Dronfield exclusive;

Staveley Control Office between Dronfield and Broad Oak Sidings exclusive;

Westhouses Control Office between Broad Oak Sidings and Alfreton;

Toton Control Office between Alfreton exclusive and Codnor Park GN Junction.

In the case of up trains, the L.N.E. Company's Control Office at Nottingham must be advised to provide an engine to work the train forward from Brinsley Junction and the L.N.E. driver of the disabled engine must conduct the L.M.S. driver from Codnor Park GN Junction to Brinsley Junction.

In the case of down trains, the L.N.E. Locomotive Department at Trafford Park must be advised to provide a conductor from the G.N. Junction to Deansgate Yard, Manchester.

Between Manchester (Deansgate) and New Mills:

In the case of failure of an L.N.E. engine working an up or down freight train between Manchester (Deansgate) and New Mills South Junction, via Cheadle Heath or via Stockport, the L.N.E. Locomotive Department at Trafford Park must be advised and the L.N.E. Company will provide an engine to work the train forward.

The working survived until 1952, latterly using Colwick J39s but still with Trafford Park men. The 8.22 p.m. departure time from Deansgate was maintained to the end, unchanged from G.N.R. days. The condition of the bridges on the connection at Codnor Park finally necessitated diversion via Woodhead. *The Railway Observer* reported that the last run was made on the night of 12th September 1952 with J39 64832.

Sources:

LNER, Great Northern Section Working Time Table, Nottingham District, 1935.

LMS, Section Appendix to Working Time Table, Midland Division, 1937.

RCTS, *The Railway Observer*, October 1952.

The Great Northern Railway, Vol. 1, John Wrottesley (Batsford, 1979).

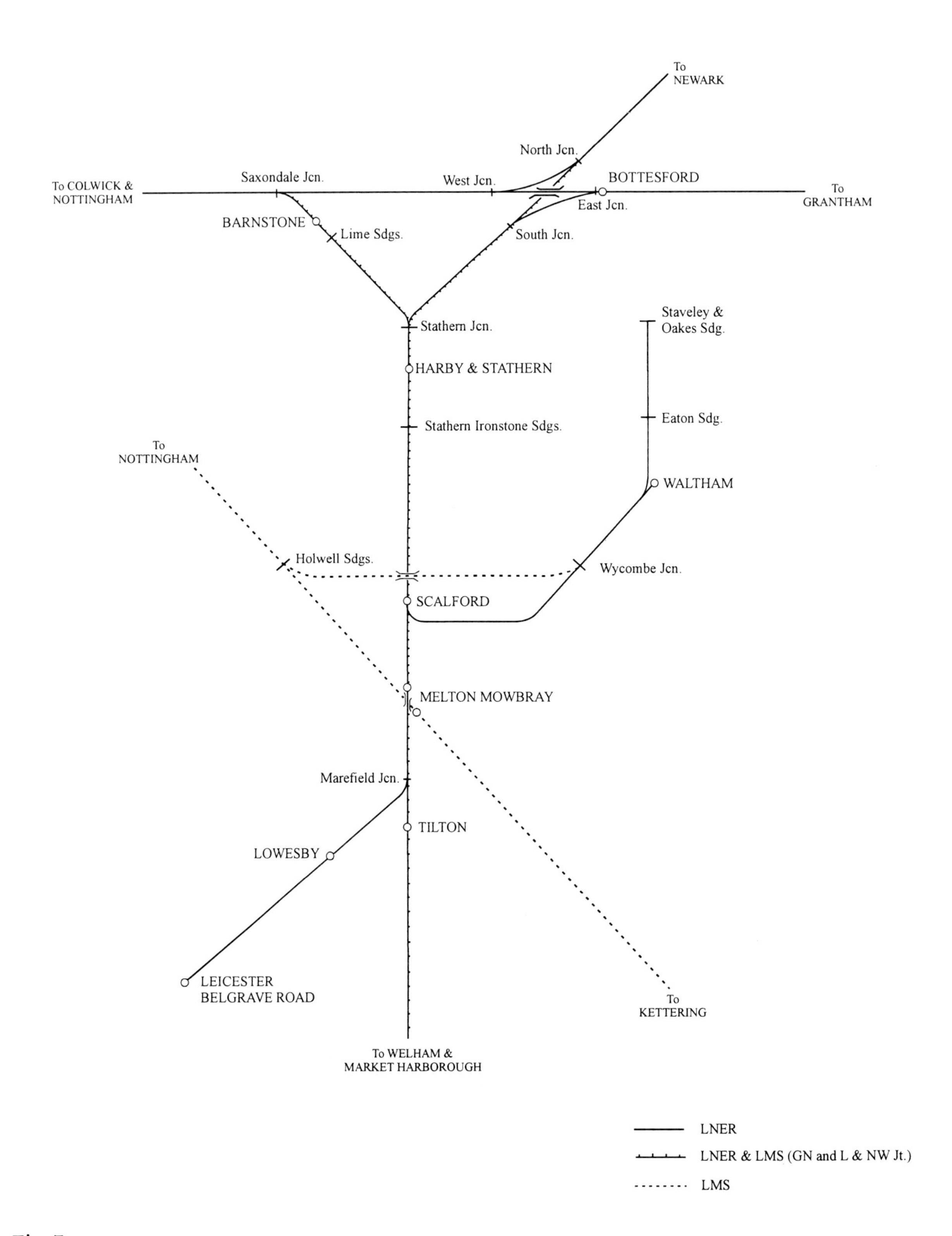
GN and L & NW JOINT RAILWAY with Associated Lines, 1935
To NEWARK
North Jcn.
To COLWICK & NOTTINGHAM
Saxondale Jcn.
West Jcn.
BOTTESFORD
To GRANTHAM
East Jcn.
BARNSTONE
Lime Sdgs.
South Jcn.
Staveley & Oakes Sdg.
Stathern Jcn.
HARBY & STATHERN
Eaton Sdg.
Stathern Ironstone Sdgs.
To NOTTINGHAM
WALTHAM
Holwell Sdgs.
Wycombe Jcn.
SCALFORD
MELTON MOWBRAY
Marefield Jcn.
TILTON
LOWESBY
LEICESTER BELGRAVE ROAD
To KETTERING
To WELHAM & MARKET HARBOROUGH
LNER
LNER & LMS (GN and L & NW Jt.)
LMS

Fig. 7

CHAPTER SIX

THE GREAT NORTHERN AND LONDON AND NORTH WESTERN JOINT RAILWAY AND ASSOCIATED LNER LINES IN 1935

LNWR Super D 0–8–0 No. 829 bringing an empty wagon train from the GN & LNW Joint line through Radcliffe. L&GRP

THE original proposal, made independently, for a line between Newark and Leicester was taken up by the Great Northern Railway in 1871. Although the Newark to Melton Mowbray section was approved by Parliament, the final portion to Leicester was rejected in the House of Lords, due to fox hunting interests, and the scheme lay dormant. But in 1872 the Midland and the Manchester Sheffield and Lincoln Railways jointly proposed a line from Rushton (near Kettering) via Melton Mowbray and Worksop to south Yorkshire. This was seen by the GNR as a serious threat to their interests. The result was a most unlikely alliance of the GNR with the London and North Western Railway, with the aim of completing the Newark and Leicester line, together with a southwards extension to Market Harborough. The proposal came to fruition as the GN and LNW Joint Railway, a title which survived the Grouping.

Authorised in 1874, the Joint Line ran northwards some 34 miles from Welham Junction near Market Harborough to Bottesford with a purely GNR extension to Newark. From Stathern Junction a joint connection to Saxondale Junction gave the LNWR access to Colwick and Nottingham. The 10¼ miles from Marefield Junction to Leicester Belgrave Road was GNR property. The LNWR had valuable running powers from Saxondale to Colwick and Nottingham and from Bottesford to Doncaster. The GNR had less useful powers from Welham to Northampton. Welham Sidings were constructed by the LNWR in 1904 just south of Welham Junction and they became a sorting point for coal which had travelled over the Joint Line. The configuration of the Joint Line and the associated LNER lines in 1935 is shown in *Fig.* 7. By then the only running powers exercised were those of the LMS from Saxondale westwards and from Wycombe Junction to the Waltham ironstone workings. The latter powers had been inherited from the Midland Railway.

Making reference to the Bill for the Joint Line, the Report of the Directors of the GNR for 15 February 1873 contains the following statement:

> "In thus agreeing with the London and North Western Company to facilitate the exchange of traffic between the respective systems, and for joint ownership in the new lines, the Directors believe, that, while dividing the responsibility of the capital expenditure involved, the two companies will secure for themselves a most valuable

K2 No. 61723 at Melton Mowbray North on 18th July 1958.

P. H. GROOM

Timber viaduct over the River Devon on the Waltham branch in 1955. C. H. A. TOWNLEY

addition to their traffic receipts, and to the public the greatest measure of accommodation possible."

As in the later case of the GN and GE Joint Line, the price paid by the GNR for the defeat of an independent incursion into its territory was the admission of a competitor by means of joint lines and running powers. The directors' forecast was not reflected by Charles Grinling 25 years later. He wrote in *The History of the Great Northern Railway*; 'The Leicestershire Joint system had established the London and North Western and the Lincolnshire the Great Eastern as formidable competitors in Great Northern districts... the Great Northern would probably have done better to have kept its money for the improvement of its own main system and to have let the promoters of the competing north-and-south lines do their worst, if direct opposition to them had not been successful.'

At the time the Leicestershire lines were built there seems to have been some over-optimism regarding traffic levels. For instance, it is difficult to imagine that, even at the peak of the railway age, full use could ever have been made of the provision for passengers at Melton Mowbray or Leicester Belgrave Road. When the 1935 Working Time Table is examined, a somewhat threadbare pattern of services is revealed; passenger workings typical of rural branches and a level of goods traffic well below the capacity of the lines concerned. The LNER was, however, very conscious of the need for economy in the working of such systems and some interesting operating practices resulted.

Before looking in detail at the LNER services of 1935, it is worth glancing at the use made of the Joint Line by the other partner. Initially, the twin goals of the LNWR were Colwick and Doncaster. The history of their workings to Doncaster is obscure. It is, however, fascinating to imagine the passage of LNWR goods trains along the GN main line from Doncaster to Newark. John Wrottesley states (ref. 1) that in 1895 vacuum-fitted wool trains were running from Bradford to Camden with GNR locomotives to Doncaster where the LNWR took over. He also states that LNWR coal trains from Doncaster had ceased by 1916 but later reappeared. At present it can only be presumed that they finally ceased during one of the strikes of the 1920s. D. L. Franks (ref. 2) gives 1910 as a year by which no LNWR trains were running to Doncaster; he mentions the Bradford to Camden wool trains with a statement that Camden drivers lodged at Doncaster on alternate trips with Whitworth class 2-4-0s, 2155 *Liver* and 2156 *Sphinx*, allotted to the working. His reference to these two locomotives is possible derived from a *Railway Magazine* article (ref. 3) which asserted that, after renewal in 1895, they were stationed at Doncaster to work these trains.

The LNWR Doncaster Shed, on the eastern side of the Carr near Red Bank, survived as a building into the days of British Railways. It was a prominent landmark, of unmistakable provenance, looking just as much an interloper on the Doncaster scene as *Liver* or *Sphinx* doubtless did in 1895. A remarkable re-embodiment of the LNWR workings was shown in the 1951 WTT when there were two Class F trains from Doncaster to Welham, at 4.9 p.m. from Mineral Yard and 7.5 p.m. from Decoy. The engine of the 7.5 p.m. turned and took water at Market Harborough, it is therefore likely that this was a Doncaster working. A return train left Northampton at 9.25 p.m. for Doncaster. By then the widespread use of Austerity 2-8-0s would probably have made the trains indistinguishable from the usual Eastern Region traffic even if the London Midland Region provided motive power. The LNWR running to Colwick had a much greater effect with a level of mineral traffic which in the early years rivalled that of the GNR. By the late 1880s some 30% of the coal despatched from Colwick was taken by the LNWR down the Joint Line. In 1935, allowing for trains designated as 'Suspended' or 'Runs when Required', some four or five Class B mineral trains ran daily from Colwick to Welham. The loaded coal trains had to contend with difficult gradients as the line rose to a summit at Tilton which was surprisingly high at 568 feet above Ordnance Datum. This involved three pitches at 1 in 120 totalling some 13½ miles of the 22 miles from Barnstone to the summit.

The LNER goods workings in 1935 were mainly concerned with general merchandise traffic for Belgrave Road and with ironstone in the Stathern district. There were, however, arrangements for exchange of traffic with the LMS at Harby and Stathern, The Working Time Table specified the guard's working by number; where these are simple out and home duties the engine workings may be taken as equivalent. This assumption has been used throughout the details which follow.

There were four daily goods arrivals at Belgrave Road, commencing at 5.25 a.m. with a Class A train, 3.28 a.m. ex Newark with a connection from Ardsley. This was followed at 6.44 a.m. by a Class B Goods and Coal which had left Colwick at 4.10 a.m. The third train was the 4.28 a.m. Class B Goods from Newark arriving at 7.18 a.m. Arrivals were completed by the 10.15 a.m. from Grantham which, despite its Class B designation, was actually a pick-up goods serving most of the intermediate stations. Arrival at Leicester was booked at 3.15 p.m. This train had a Leicester guard whose outward working was the 7.10 a.m. passenger to Grantham. It is possible that the engine working was similar. Class 3 engines, i.e. J6, were specified for the first two trains; power for the remaining two was not mentioned.

Departures from Belgrave Road commenced with the 8.45 a.m. Class B to Colwick with a J6; this was the return working of the 4.10 a.m. from Colwick. At 9.15 p.m. a goods left for Newark with traffic for Yorkshire, North Eastern stations and Scotland. Due at Newark at 11.0 p.m. it was noted as Speed 2 in the WWT, i.e. a No 2 Braked Goods although its booked times were scarcely an improvement on those given to the Class A and B trains. It was a Leicester J6 working, returning with the 3.28 a.m. from Newark. The 9.15 p.m. was followed out of Belgrave Road by another No 2 Braked Goods at 9.35 p.m. for Colwick, arriving there at 10.57 p.m. The guard had already been in charge of the 6.40 p.m. passenger to Lowesby and its return to Belgrave Road. How he reached Leicester initially is not recorded. There was also a balancing working for the 4.28 a.m. from Newark which was noted as 'Returns from Leicester as ordered by Control'.

Marshalling of this by no means heavy traffic nominally occupied a Yard Pilot at Belgrave Road from 6.0 a.m. to 10.0 p.m. The engine from the passenger train arriving at 9.6 a.m. relieved the pilot while the latter made a trip to Humberstone and shunted the yard there.

The line between Bottesford South and North Junctions giving direct running between Leicester and Newark was used only by three up and two down booked goods trains, all passing during the night, the first at 10.41 p.m. and the last at 4.49 a.m. Bottesford North Junction Box was open for these trains from 9.45 p.m. to 5.15 a.m. each night. During the day from 5.15 a.m. to 9.45 p.m. its points were set for the spur to the West Junction for use by the daytime Colwick to Newark traffic. The passenger service from Leicester to Grantham, together with the one Grantham to Leicester pick-up goods, used the South Junction to East Junction spur, the first and last trains passing at 7.48 a.m. and 7.21 p.m. respectively. It was therefore possible to close the South Junction Box as a block post, the points being set for running to the North Junction during the night when that box was open and for the East Junction during the day. It is perhaps significant that the North Box was open for 7½ hours; a reasonable assumption is that the North signalman began and ended his shift by re-setting the points, and operating switches to transfer the block indications accordingly, at the South Box just over ½ mile distant. It will be seen that the return working of the 4.28 a.m. Newark to Leicester train, referred to above, would have to be made at a time when its route at Bottesford was nominally unavailable. From 5.15 a.m. the points at Bottesford South Junction were set for the line to Grantham and the North Junction box was closed with the points set for the Nottingham to Newark route. The answer to this problem has been provided by Mr Ron Woodcock, at one time a signalman at Bottesford East. 'Control' would advise Bottesford East when the Leicester to Newark route was required for a train in the daytime. The East box would be closed temporarily and the signalman walked to the South and North boxes in turn, setting the road for Newark at the South and opening the North box to deal with the train. He then walked back by the same route, resetting the road for Grantham at the South box. This could happen two or three times in a shift, involving much walking in all weathers.

In addition to the Leicester trains there was a daily Class D Pick-up Goods from Colwick to Melton Mowbray and return. This left Carlton Field with a Class 2 (J3) engine at 11.10 a.m. and was due to arrive back at Colwick at 8.21 p.m. The outward and homeward guard's duty numbers were different so it is likely that the first set of men were relieved at Melton. On Tuesday (Melton market) this train was supplemented by a No. 2 Braked Cattle from Melton Mowbray at 3.2 p.m. to Colwick. The J3 for this working ran light engine from Colwick at 10.50 a.m.

The LMS still sent some traffic for Doncaster over the Joint Line and this was exchanged with the LNER at Harby and Stathern. An LNER working from Doncaster was provided, leaving Doncaster Mineral, with a J6 as a Class B Goods and Coal, at 7.25 p.m. and arriving at Harby and Stathern at 1.24 a.m. The return commenced at 3.20 a.m., arriving at Mineral at 8.0 a.m. There were lengthy stops at Newark in each direction and it is likely that re-manning took place there.

Three workings from Colwick to the Stathern ironstone district remain to be described. The first left Colwick at 7.30 a.m. taking empty wagons to Stathern Ironstone Sidings, arriving at 8.19 a.m. The engine (J6) and brake then returned to Harby and Stathern, leaving there at 9.50 a.m. as a Class B Goods and Empties to Barnstone Lime Siding and Barnstone. Engine and brake returned from Barnstone to Stathern Ironstone Sidings, finally leaving with a Class C Mineral load at 12.35 p.m. for Colwick, arriving back at Locomotive Junction at 1.20 p.m. The purpose of the curious intermediate trip was to work Barnstone Lime Siding which was connected to the down line only. The single line Waltham branch was worked from Colwick by a trip leaving there at 8.15 a.m. for Scalford hauled by a J6. The working on the branch is described later. Scalford was left at 2.46 p.m. with a Class C Mineral load to arrive at Colwick at 4.57 p.m. The final train was the only one on the Joint Line to require a large LNER engine. An O4 left Colwick at 11.40 a.m. with a Class B Goods and Empties for Stathern Ironstone Sidings, arriving at 12.56 p.m. The return commenced at 3.20 p.m. as a Class C Mineral with a maximum load of 45 10-ton wagons and a 20-ton brake. A stop was made at Netherfield for water and trainmen's relief. The second set of men continued at 4.32 p.m. via Nottingham Victoria and the GCR main line to Staveley Works, arriving at 7.46 p.m. The outward run was made tender first because the O4 was too long for the 45ft turntable at Harby and Stathern.

The only train to use the section between Scalford and Wycombe Junction was the 8.15 a.m. from Colwick on its round trip on the Waltham Branch. A simple Train Staff sufficed for its protection between these points. Its presence on the section from Wycombe Junction to Waltham, however, gave rise to a daily change in the working regulations. Although it was an LNER branch, the chief user was the LMS under running powers. Three of the four daily LMS trains from Holwell Sidings had sole use of the line from Wycombe Junction in accordance with Appendix III of the Regulations for Working Single Lines of Railway (One Engine in Steam). At 11.5 a.m. the LNER train followed the 10.24 a.m. LMS train from Wycombe to Waltham so from 10.24 a.m. to when both trains had cleared Wycombe Junction on their return the line was worked under Appendix II of the regulations (Working by Pilot Guard). The Pilot Guard would despatch the 10.24 a.m. from Wycombe Junction with a 'Pilot Guard's Ticket', travel to Waltham by the LNER train at 11.5 a.m. and, on arrival there, despatch the LMS train back to Wycombe Junction with another ticket. The LNER goods travelled on to Eaton Siding and, if required, penetrated to the remote reaches of Staveley and Oakes

No. 43032 near Stathern Junction with the 1.45 p.m. ex-Leicester Belgrave Road on 8th September 1962. This was the last goods to use the line between Stathern Junction and Saxondale Junction. T. G. HEPBURN

Ironstone Siding. On arrival back at Wycombe Junction at 2.33 p.m. with the Pilot Guard, the working reverted to 'One Engine in Steam' for the remainder of the day. The Pilot Guard operated the boxes at Wycombe Junction and Waltham-on-the-Wold as required, thereby replacing two signalmen. This most unusual change of regulations in the course of the day was possibly unique. In GNR days working was by Train Staff and Ticket, and excursion trains could carry passengers to Waltham for Croxton Park Races. A surviving Notice for 4th April 1889 shows five such trains, plus one conditional, from Nottingham, one from Newark and Grantham, one from Leicester and one from Northampton, all arriving at Waltham between 11.6 a.m. and 2.17 p.m. Incidentally, the same Notice gives the times of an LNWR excursion to Lincoln from Higham Ferrers (later Irthlingborough) and Northampton via the Joint line, Allington Junction and Honington, LNWR engine throughout, GNR pilot-man from Bottesford.

Returning to 1935, a summary of the approximate total numbers of trains which traversed the various sections daily is given below:

Section	*LNER Pass'r*	*LNER Goods*	*LMS Pass'r*	*LMS Goods*	*Total*
Bottesford North Jc. to Bottesford South Jc.	–	5	–	–	5
Bottesford South Jc. to Stathern	10	6	–	–	16
Saxondale Jc. to Stathern	–	11	10	9	30
Stathern to Melton Mowbray	10	9	10	9	38
Melton Mowbray, Marefield and Leicester	10	7	–	–	17
Melton Mowbray, Marefield and Welham	–	–	10	11	21

It is interesting to note that LNER goods trains outnumbered those of the LMS on the Saxondale to Stathern connection which had been added to the original scheme solely for the convenience of the LNWR. This was due to LNER traffic in ironstone, the deposits of which had first attracted the independent promoters of the Newark to Leicester line.

Ten passenger trains in each direction through Melton Mowbray gives an impression of prosperity, but in reality this was the confluence of the uninspired all stations services from Leicester to Grantham (LNER) and Northampton to Nottingham (LMS). The former dwindled rapidly under wartime conditions and never recovered. An arrival at Nottingham from Melton on the latter is remembered with London Road Low Level devoid of staff to collect tickets and only a handful of passengers, mostly railwaymen, alighting. Belgrave Road came alive briefly on summer Saturdays but the East Coast season is short and such occasions did little to outweigh the general somnolence. The unavoidable conclusion is that Grinling's strictures of 1898 were a truer forecast of the future than the optimism of the Great Northern directors in 1873.

References:
1. John Wrottesley, *The Great Northern Railway, Vol. III,* (Batsford, 1981) pp. 144 and 164.
2. D. L. Franks, *Great Northern and London and North West Joint Railway* (1974)
3. C. J. Alcock, 'A Famous Identity Locomotive Class', *Railway Magazine* Jan. 1919.

Sources:
LNER, Great Northern Section Working Time Table, Nottingham District (Summer 1935)
Great Northern Railway, Directors' Reports (1873)
Charles H. Grinling, *The History of the Great Northern Railway* (1898).

CHAPTER SEVEN

WOODFORD AND HINTON IN 1939

Unusual motive power for a Class C train, C4 No. 6094 at Saunderton. H. E. SIMMONS

'Is Woodford church or Hinton church
The one I ought to see?
Or were they both too much restored
In 1883?
I do not know. Towards the west
A trail of glory runs
And we leave the old Great Central line
For Banbury and buns'

BETJEMAN unerringly sets the scene. Woodford and Hinton was situated deep in rural England, but occupied a vital position on the Great Central's extension to London. Later to be renamed Woodford Halse, it will be referred to hereafter simply as Woodford.

The Great Northern, at Peterborough, and the Midland, at Wellingborough, had established staging posts for mineral traffic, roughly half-way between the coalfields and London. The Great Central followed suit at Woodford. Here, the choice of location as a mid-point on the new route to the Capital was reinforced by the proximity of the junction at Culworth, less than two miles to the south, where the line to Banbury diverged. Despite the original grandiose aims of the London Extension, it was this connection to Banbury which carried the greater part of the goods and mineral traffic that passed through Woodford. Banbury was indeed a gateway to the whole of the south-west from the Great Central line.

Fig. 8 shows the connections from Woodford to the south, including the spur to the Stratford-upon-Avon and Midland Junction section of the LMS. It also shows the various minor lines which criss-crossed the sparsely populated countryside. At Grendon Underwood Junction, the Extension split into connections to the Great Western and Great Central Joint line and to the Metropolitan and Great Central Joint line to reach London via High Wycombe and Aylesbury respectively. The Aylesbury route was 4½ miles shorter but was more severely graded. In addition to its easier gradients, a further advantage of the Wycombe route for goods traffic was the provision of up and down running loops at ten locations. Some of these loops, however, were short, primarily serving station platforms. The Aylesbury route had only a limited number of refuge sidings.

Whichever direction was taken at Grendon Underwood, however, trains from Woodford had to be fitted into independent traffic flows. Via Wycombe, the Great Western's Birmingham line was shared for about 34 miles between Ashendon Junction and Northolt Junction East. Between Rickmansworth and Harrow on the Aylesbury route, all traffic, including the Metropolitan electric trains, used one pair of lines. The limitations resulted in a stern operating injunction:

WORKING OF FREIGHT TRAINS BETWEEN WOODFORD AND NEASDEN

'The booked train times, except in unavoidable circumstances, must be rigidly adhered to. Should, however, it be found impossible to start the mineral or mineral empty trains from either end at the times shown,

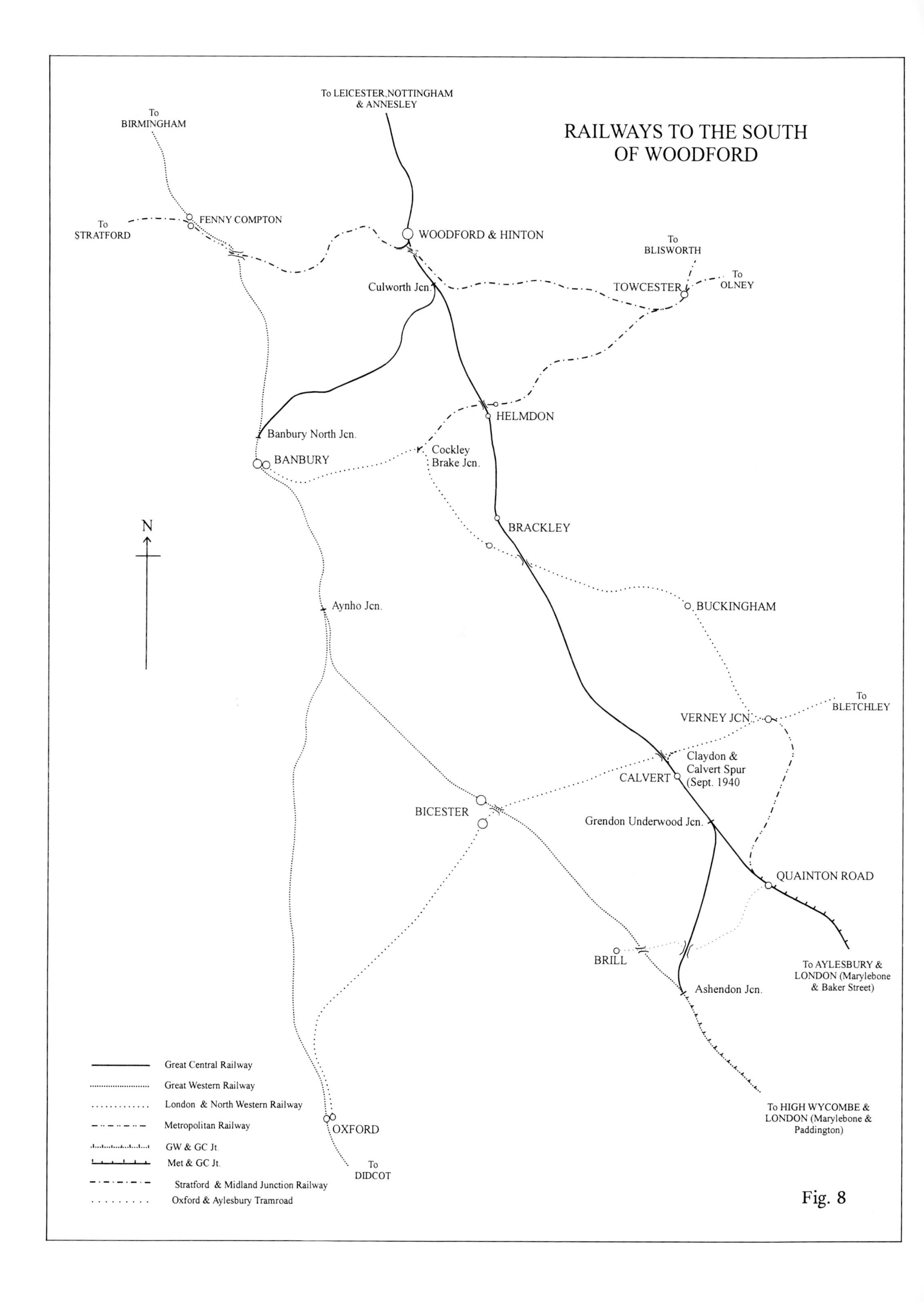
RAILWAYS TO THE SOUTH OF WOODFORD
To LEICESTER,NOTTINGHAM & ANNESLEY
To BIRMINGHAM
To STRATFORD
FENNY COMPTON
WOODFORD & HINTON
To BLISWORTH
To OLNEY
TOWCESTER
Culworth Jcn.
HELMDON
Banbury North Jcn.
BANBURY
Cockley Brake Jcn.
N
BRACKLEY
BUCKINGHAM
Aynho Jcn.
To BLETCHLEY
VERNEY JCN.
Claydon & Calvert Spur (Sept. 1940
CALVERT
BICESTER
Grendon Underwood Jcn.
QUAINTON ROAD
BRILL
To AYLESBURY & LONDON (Marylebone & Baker Street)
Ashendon Jcn.
To HIGH WYCOMBE & LONDON (Marylebone & Paddington)
OXFORD
To DIDCOT
Great Central Railway
Great Western Railway
London & North Western Railway
Metropolitan Railway
GW & GC Jt.
Met & GC Jt.
Stratford & Midland Junction Railway
Oxford & Aylesbury Tramroad

Fig. 8

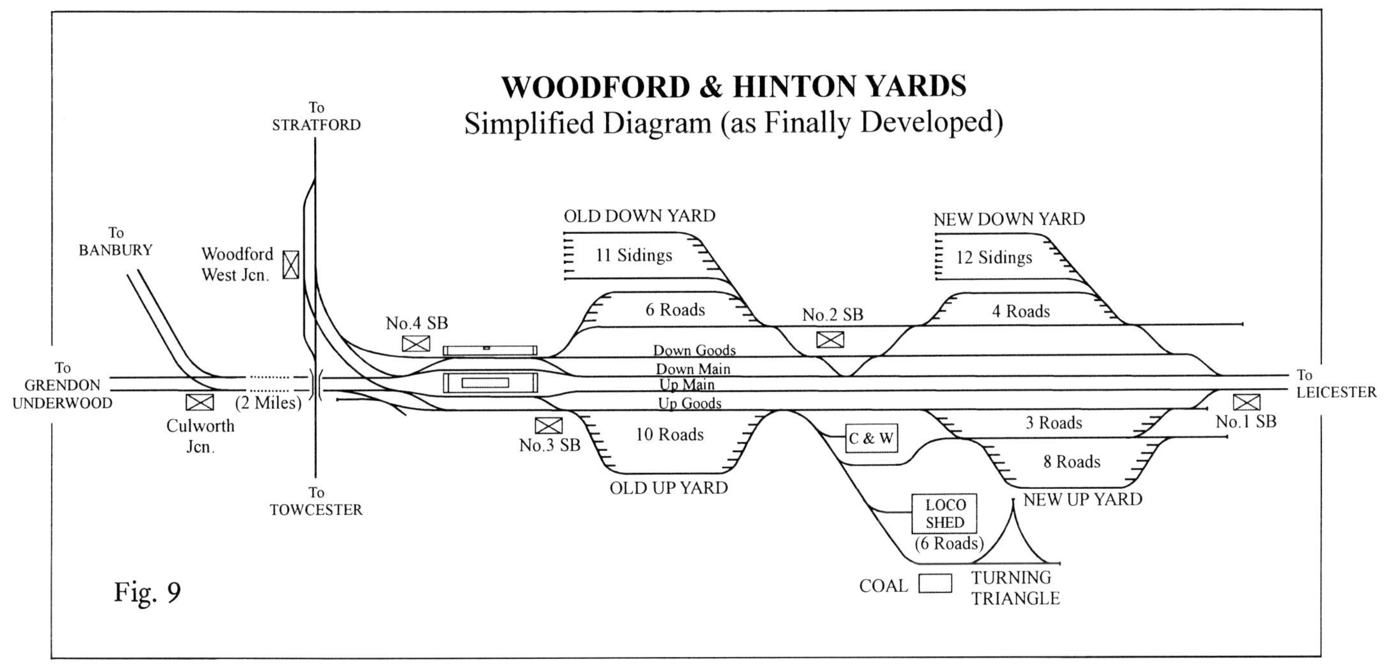

Woodford shed in 1935. All the locomotives visible were of Great Central design. L&GRP

then such trains must be put back to the immediately following booked service or the alternative path, and the line throughout to destination must be advised of the alternative.

'The trains must be despatched from Woodford or Neasden respectively at their booked times, and the alternative paths must only be used when absolutely necessary. Any special train which it may be necessary to run between Woodford and Neasden in either direction must be run in one of the booked paths.'

This notice appeared in the Summer 1939 WTT. The demands of wartime probably led to the introduction of more flexible arrangements. Certainly the capacity of the line to the north of Woodford was stretched to its limit during World War 2. Although there were few changes southwards to London, the war brought significant improvements to the Nottingham–Woodford section. New up and down loops were installed at Ruddington, Loughborough, Swithland and Ashby Magna with additional loops in the more critical up direction at Quorn, Rugby and Charwelton. At Woodford, the capacity of the yards was approximately doubled by the provision of the new up and down yards to the north of the original installations. A further wartime innovation was the replacement of the original 54ft diameter turntable by a reversing triangle. The final development of Woodford is shown in *Fig. 9*. Of the four main line signal boxes, No. 1 was a new provision, No. 2 was originally known as North Loop Junction and No. 4 was originally known as Central. Only No. 3 remained unchanged in

O4 No. 6221 with an up Class C goods at Charwelton on 3rd July 1937. L. HANSON

designation. No. 2 box had a 75-lever frame with only two spares. The frame in No. 4 could accommodate 76 levers but there were twelve spaces. Simplifications and replacement of the fouling bars by track circuits had increased the number of spare levers to eighteen by 1960.

In the post-war period, traffic was dealt with in the yards as follows:

Old Up Yard:	Up traffic except that for the Banbury line.
New Up Yard:	Banbury traffic.
Old Down Yard:	All down loaded traffic.
New Down Yard:	All empties:

In 1939, with the line basically in the same condition as when it was built, the only running loops between the Trent bridge at Nottingham and Woodford were at Leicester where they were provided both at the passenger and goods stations. There was, perforce, much shunting of goods trains into refuge sidings. Some improvements had, however, been made to the signalling. In the up direction, the long 1 in 176 climbs resulted in protracted section times for heavy loaded coal trains. As early as 1907, the GCR had found it necessary to install semi-automatic signals to break the section of 4 miles 867 yards from Whetstone to Ashby Magna. By 1939, also on the up line only, intermediate block signals had been provided between Staverton Road and Charwelton. In the latter section the line climbed through Catesby tunnel to a summit 503 feet above sea level.

O4 No. 6537 with a Woodford to Annesley empty wagon train at Charwelton on 3rd July 1937. L. HANSON

J39 No. 2982 with an up No. 2 express goods at Charwelton on 3rd July 1937. L. HANSON

Tables 14 & 15 show the up and down goods trains which passed through Woodford on weekdays in the summer of 1939. All remaining workings were regarded as either commencing or terminating there. *Table 16* shows the total number of weekday trains of various classes using each of the three routes to the south and also the main line to the north.

South of Grendon Underwood most of the Marylebone express passenger workings used the Aylesbury route. Apart from passenger trains, the portion between Grendon Underwood and Quainton Road was used only by two down No. 2 braked goods, a milk train which is referred to later and two local workings in each direction between Woodford and Quainton Road. There was still

TABLE 14
WOODFORD – UP THROUGH GOODS TRAINS – TUESDAYS TO FRIDAYS, SUMMER 1939

Class	*From*	*dep.*	*Woodford arr.*	*Woodford dep.*	*Destination*	*arr.*	*Route*
No. 1 Braked	Doncaster	8.17 p.m.	pass 12.15 a.m.		Banbury	12.35 a.m.	Tuxford, Mansfield
No. 2 Braked	Sheffield, Bridgehouses	9.16 p.m.	1.9 a.m.	1.30 a.m.	Banbury Junction	1.55 a.m.	Staveley
No. 1 Braked	Ardwick East	7.50 p.m.	1.35 a.m.	2.3 a.m.	Marlyebone Goods	4.0 a.m.	Shirebrook, High Wycombe
No. 1 Braked	Godley	9.23 p.m.	3.5 a.m.	4.14 a.m.	Marlyebone Goods	6.25 a.m.	Shirebrook, High Wycombe
No. 2 Braked	Stairfoot	7.20 p.m.	3.43 a.m.	4.20 a.m.	Banbury Junction	4.45 a.m.	Shirebrook
No. 1 Braked	York, Severus	11.40 p.m.	4.41 a.m.	4.59 a.m.	Marlyebone Goods	6.50 a.m.	Darnall, Staveley, High Wycombe
No. 1 Braked	York, Dringhouses	12.35 a.m.	5.1 a.m.	5.19 a.m.	Marlyebone Goods	7.8 a.m.	Tuxford, Mansfield High Wycombe
No. 2 Braked	Ardwick East	9.5 p.m.	5.43 a.m.	6.30 a.m.	Marlyebone Goods	10.15 a.m.	Staveley, High Wycombe
No. 1 Braked	Doncaster Decoy	3.32 p.m.	pass 7.8 p.m.		Banbury	7.58 p.m.	Tuxford, Mansfield
Class A	Leicester	9.35 p.m.	10.51 p.m.	11.17 p.m.	Banbury Junction	11.42 p.m.	–
Class A	Mansfield	7.0 p.m.	11.11 p.m.	11.43 p.m.	Banbury Junction	12.8 a.m.	–
No. 1 Braked	Grimsby	6.27 p.m.	pass 11.37 p.m.		Banbury	12.1 a.m.	Tuxford, Mansfield

TABLE 15
WOODFORD – DOWN THROUGH GOODS TRAINS – TUESDAYS TO FRIDAYS, SUMMER 1939

Class	*From*	*dep.*	*Woodford arr.*	*Woodford dep.*	*Destination*	*arr.*	*Route*
No. 1 Braked	Marylebone Goods	9.50 p.m.	pass 12.7 a.m.		Ardwick East		High Wycombe, Staveley
No. 2 Braked	Marylebone Goods	10.20 p.m.	12.52 a.m.	2.0 a.m.	Mottram		Aylesbury, Shirebrook
No. 2 Braked	Marylebone Goods	11.20 p.m.	1.57 a.m.	2.55 a.m.	Sheffield, Bernard Road	1.45 a.m.	Staveley
No. 1 Braked	Banbury	4.5 a.m.	pass 4.23 a.m.		Sheffield, Victoria	7.23 a.m.	Staveley
Class A	Banbury Junction	6.25 a.m.	6.52 a.m.	7.5 a.m.	Sheffield, Bernard Road	1.45 p.m.	Staveley
No. 2 Braked	Neasden	9.40 a.m.	12.36 p.m.	1.52 p.m.	Wadsley Braidge		High Wycombe, Staveley
No. 1 Braked	Banbury	6.5 p.m.	pass 6.22 p.m.		York		Staveley, Darnall
No. 1 Braked	Banbury Junction	9.7 p.m.	9.30 p.m.	9.55 p.m.	Stainforth		Shirebrook, Darnall

TABLE 16
SUMMARY OF GOODS TRAFFIC AT WOODFORD TUESDAYS TO FRIDAYS, SUMMER 1939

UP

Class of Train	*From the North to Woodford*	*Woodford to Banbury*	*Woodford to the Aylesbury line*	*Woodford to the Wycombe line*
No. 1 Braked	7	3	–	4
No. 2 Braked	3	3	–	2
Class A	9	2	–	–
Class B	1	–	1	–
Class C	14	13	–	4
Class D	1	–	1	1
Total	35	21	2	11

DOWN

Class of train	*Woodford to the North*	*Banbury to Woodford*	*Aylesbury line to Woodford*	*Wycombe line to Woodford*
No. 1 Braked	4	3	–	1
No. 2 Braked	4	–	2	1
Class A	10	4	–	1
Class B	–	–	–	1
Class C	16	13	2	2
Class D	1	–	–	1
Total	35	20	4	7

O4 No. 6316 with an up coal train in 1946 climbing at 1 in 176 at Staverton Road box between Braunston and Charwelton. J. A. G. H. COLTAS

B7 No. 1380 (5472 pre-1946) heading an up coal train at Staverton Road in 1947. J. A. G. H. COLTAS

careful division of local goods trains into those serving the LNER proper and those serving the Metropolitan and Great Central Joint. The Quainton Road trains are readily identifiable as Woodford workings:

	arr.	*dep.*	*arr.*	*dep.*
Woodford		3.0 a.m.		3.25 p.m.
	Class B Goods		Class D Goods	
Quainton Road	4.3 a.m.	6.10 a.m.	7.15 p.m.	
	Engine and Brake			
Aylesbury	6.20 a.m.	8.50 a.m.		
	Engine and Brake			
Quainton Road	9.2 a.m.	9.55 a.m.		8.3 p.m.
	Class C Empties		Class C Empties	
Woodford	11.15 a.m.		9.23 p.m.	

The morning trip was non-stop in each direction between Woodford and Quainton Road. The 3.25 p.m. called at the intermediate stations, the through load being limited to 35 wagons in addition to the roadside traffic. The return trip called at Calvert only.

The two down No. 2 braked trains left Marylebone Goods at 10.20 p.m. and 11.20 p.m. for Mottram and Sheffield respectively. The 10.20 p.m. stopped at Aylesbury for 22 minutes. Its load over the Chilterns was 35 wagons – 'if worked by a four-cylinder engine (i.e. a B7), 5 wagons more'. It could convey 45 wagons between Aylesbury and Nottingham – 'and when doing so will be allowed 8 minutes extra running time'. After following the

10.5 p.m. to Manchester out of Marylebone it was passed at Aylesbury by the 10.45 p.m. Marylebone to Newcastle. This was the cheap fare train which later in its journey was taken through by a Leicester B17 from its home station to Newcastle, alternating with a Gateshead K3. These four trains must have provided noisy bedtimes for Metrolanders who lived near the 1 in 105 climb to Amersham.

As an aside from goods traffic, the night trains to the North East coast must have carried a fair proportion of the long distance passengers using Marylebone at the time. In addition to the 10.45 p.m. via Aylesbury, there was a conditional path for a 10.30 p.m. via Wycombe on Mondays to Fridays. On Saturday night the goods workings were reduced to a 9.45 p.m. from Marylebone Goods to Sheffield via Aylesbury. This train was followed by Newcastle passengers at 10.30 and 10.45 p.m. via Wycombe and the Manchester mail at 11.0 p.m. and a third Newcastle at 11.26 p.m., both via Aylesbury. The

O1 No. 3476 with an up Class C goods train at Staverton Road in 1946.
J. A. G. H. COLTAS

A down empty wagon train at Staverton Road in 1946 hauled by J11 No. 5328. J. A. G. H. COLTAS

10.45 was booked to stand for 11 minutes at Grendon Underwood to allow the 11.0 p.m. to proceed.

The Wycombe route was served by daily Class D pick-up trains in each direction between Woodford and Neasden. Calling at all yards from Calvert to Ruislip, the 5.35 a.m. from Woodford did not reach Neasden until 3.12 p.m. In the down direction, the 4.5 a.m. from Neasden called at all yards from Denham northwards. It was booked to arrive at Woodford at 12.17 p.m.

The details of four No. 1 braked trains to Marylebone Goods via Wycombe are shown in *Table 14*. The loads of the two trains from York which head the table were both limited to 35 fully braked wagons south of Woodford when hauled by a B7. North of Woodford, the 11.40 p.m. from Severus could comprise up to 45 wagons unassisted. For loads between 45 and 50 wagons a pilot was provided between Tinsley and Nottingham. If the load exceeded 50 wagons, the train was assisted throughout from Doncaster to Woodford. The 12.35 a.m. could take up to 50 wagons when hauled by a K3. This could be extended to 60 wagons with a pilot from Doncaster to Woodford. There were two No. 2 braked trains from Woodford via Wycombe. The 12.33 a.m. commenced at Woodford and, after short stops at Wycombe and Neasden, reached Marylebone Goods at 3.45 a.m. The 9.5 p.m. from Ardwick East was nominally a through train, although a stop of over two hours at Annesley probably indicates extensive re-marshalling. Two up passenger trains passed it at Gerrards Cross and, with a stop at Neasden, Marylebone Goods was not reached until 10.15 a.m.

There were only two down braked trains via Wycombe. The 9.40 a.m. empties from Neasden to Wadsley Bridge ran as a No. 2 braked goods. The 9.50 p.m. from Marylebone Goods to Ardwick East was a No. 1 braked train with a load limited to 38 wagons. It ran non-stop to Leicester.

Mineral traffic to Neasden was conveyed by four Class C trains, leaving Woodford at 7.50 a.m. and 5.56, 9.05 and 10.15 p.m. Four conditional paths were also provided. For all these trains there was a booked stop at Princes Risborough for water. Various additional stops were also made, either for detaching or to keep clear of faster traffic. The best overall time from Woodford to Neasden was 4 hours 27 minutes, this being at night with a reasonably clear road. As with all the other Class C trains on the Great Central section at the time, haulage would largely be handled by the Robinson O4 2-8-0s. The empty workings were varied. The 12.40 a.m. Class B from Marylebone Goods made up its load at Neasden with empty wagons. The 7.56 p.m. from Neasden ran as Class A with a load limited, as far as High Wycombe, to 35 wagons. Finally, there were two Class C trains from Neasden at 3.15 and 4.35 a.m. Two conditional paths were also laid down.

The working of mineral trains on the line to Banbury was performed largely by pilot engines from Woodford. The distance to Banbury Junction where goods traffic was exchanged with the GWR was only ten miles. Engines worked through from the north with passenger and through goods trains. The exchange with the GWR of the former and some of the latter took place at Banbury station, just over 11 miles from Woodford.

The three No. 1 braked fish trains all ran through to Banbury station without a Woodford stop. The first of these, the 3.32 p.m. from Doncaster Decoy, was K3-hauled with a load of 45 vans. The 6.27 p.m. from Grimsby was headed by a B1 with a load limited to 37 vans. In 1939 the B1 classification applied to Nos. 5195/6, the first two 4-6-0s built for the Great Central Railway, both then allocated to Woodford. They were re-classified B18 in 1943 to make way for the Thompson B1s. From Banbury, the engine worked back to Woodford at 1.10 a.m. with a Class A goods. In the 1939 WTT, the third train, at 8.17 p.m. from Doncaster, was still designated for B17 haulage with 40 vans. The three engines of this class, No. 2832, 2833 and 2835, which had shared the working of the train up to 1938, had, however, been transferred to the Great Eastern section. It is likely that V2s were used in 1939.

The fish traffic was balanced by three down No. 1 braked trains. An engine ran light from Woodford to take the 6.5 p.m. fruit and vegetable train from Banbury Junction. A second engine worked a passenger train from Woodford to Banbury and then ran back light to Banbury Junction to take the 9.7 p.m. fish empties northward. The third train carried perishables to Sheffield, leaving Banbury station at 4.5 a.m. Three No. 2 braked goods and two Class A goods worked through to Banbury Junction in the up direction. There was only a single through Class A train in the down direction to balance them. This was the 6.25 a.m. from Banbury Junction to Sheffield. It was worked by the engine which arrived at 4.5 a.m. with the 7.20 p.m. from Stairfoot.

Six pilot engines were provided daily by Woodford shed. Nos. 1 and 2 were triple-manned shunting pilots and, apart from 1½ hours attention on shed, were available throughout the 24 hours, No. 1 on the down side and No. 2 on the up. No. 2 relieved No. 1 during the latter's shed time and also shunted the Carriage and Wagon shops and the Loco Coal sidings. Nos. 3, 5 & 6 pilots worked the mineral trips to Banbury Junction, making 5, 4 and 4 return trips respectively. No. 4 looked after the passenger stations and goods yard and the workings round the spur to the SMJ. These comprised three return passenger trips by Byfield and two transfer goods trips to Woodford West Junction. During a typical 24 hours, 46 light engines left Woodford shed to work outward trains.

The trains which ran through Woodford to or from the north have already been noted. Up goods working terminating at Woodford comprised three Class A, one Class B and one Class D trains. The Class A trains were the 2.10 a.m. and the 4.30 p.m. from York Dringhouses,

O4 No. 6262 with a Class D pick-up goods on Charwelton troughs.
H. GORDON TIDEY

both running via Darnall and Staveley, and the 9.5 p.m. from Annesley. The Class B goods was nominally a through working from Hull, leaving at 10.0 p.m. but it spent over three hours at Annesley. The Class D pick-up left Leicester at 6.3 a.m. and reached Woodford 6½ hours later after having called at all the intermediate yards. Down goods trains originating at Woodford included a No. 2 braked working at 7.20 a.m. to York and from Class A goods, at 3.20 a.m. for Grimsby, 11.45 a.m. for York, 6.40 p.m. for Leicester (continuing to York as a No. 2 braked train) and 8.30 p.m. to Hull. The 3.20 a.m. to Grimsby ran via Mansfield and Tuxford, all the others being routed via Staveley and Darnall. The down Class D pick-up left at 6.42 a.m. and was due to arrive at Leicester at 12.33 p.m.

Four Class A mineral trains ran to and from Annesley and there were also fourteen and sixteen down Class C mineral workings, the latter mostly consisting of empty wagons. The fourteen up Class C trains originated at various locations. Seven started from Annesley and two from Bulwell Common. In both the latter cases the engine ran light from Annesley to pick up the train. Of the remainder, two were from Warsop Junction and one each from Sheffield, Worksop and Frodingham. The best journey times from Annesley for these trains, mostly hauled by O4s, were just under 4½ hours. This included a booked stop for water at Rugby and at least one stand for other trains to pass. The actual running time was about 3¾ hours. The lighter down trains were allowed much the same times, in some cases with a booked stop for water at Loughborough. Such times did not permit an out and home working to Woodford for the Annesley trainmen. In 1932, the LNER had initiated Class A mineral workings between New England and Ferme Park in order to secure better utilisation of engine and men. Similar trains were introduced from Annesley in the next year. Special arrangements were made for a quick turn-round for the men on arrival at Woodford. The timetable for the four return journeys made daily in 1939 was:

		a.m.	*a.m.*	*p.m.*	*p.m.*
Annesley	dep	1.40	8.30	12.20	6.15
Loughborough	arr	-	-	-	7.17
-	dep	-	-	-	7.33
Leicester Passenger	arr	3. 2	9.55	1.44	8. 1
-	dep	3. 8	10. 3	1.50	8. 9
Woodford	arr	4.33	11.28	3.35	9.34
		a.m.	*a.m.*	*p.m.*	*p.m.*
Woodford	dep	6.20	12.15	4.40	11. 2
					a.m.
Leicester Goods	arr	-	1.19	-	12. 6
-	dep	-	1.43	-	12.26
Nottingham Victoria	arr	-	-	6.40	-
-	dep	-	-	6.47	-
Annesley	arr	8.55	3.10	7.22	1.56

At first, in 1933, these trains were hauled by B7s or B8s but the latter were soon replaced by K3s. In 1939, the designated load for a B7 or K3 was fifty 10 ton wagons of minerals and a 20 ton brake van. Going back with the empties, the number of wagons was increased to fifty-five. On the up run, a stop for water was made at Leicester; the troughs on the Extension at Charwelton were positioned to suit the Marylebone expresses and were too near Woodford to be of use to the mineral workings. Times between the arrival and departure of trains at Woodford ranged from 47 to 107 minutes. Woodford men took over the incoming engine and brought out another for the return journey.

The best up running time for the 66.28 miles was 167 minutes, an average of 23.8 mph. Going back without a water stop, the 6.20 a.m. from Woodford achieved a time of 155 minutes, an average of 25.7 mph. Compared with

B7 No. 5078 heading a Class C train through the deep cutting at Saunderton where up and down lines diverge for a short distance.

H. E. SIMMONS

D11 No. 5504 Jutland *with the Dorrington milk empties, 2.9 p.m. from Marylebone, at Harrow.* C. R. L. COLES

B7 No. 5473 on Neasden shed yard on 9th October 1937. G. T. STAMP

the ruling gradient of 1 in 200 faced by the Class A workings from New England to Ferme Park, the loaded trains from Annesley had to be eased down the long initial 1 in 132 drop towards Nottingham and cope with a ruling gradient of 1 in 176 thereafter. Brake power as well as tractive effort was a factor in the operation.

After wartime interruption, the out and home workings from Annesley were resumed in 1947. Traffic had increased during the war and no less than 31 trains were involved. The timings were now somewhat easier and, to ensure completion of a turn within eight hours, the crews booked on at Bulwell Common, taking over there from pilot crews who brought the trains from Annesley. O4s were used at first, soon to be replaced by Thompson O1s. In addition to the new running loops, eight up and three down intermediate block signals had been installed. In 1953, some headways were as short as ten minutes and typical overall times were 3¼ to 3¾ hours.

Eventually, the workings were taken over by brand new 9F 2-10-0s. The timings were accelerated to 2½-2¾ hours up and about 2¼ hours down. This enabled the crew change at Bulwell Common to be eliminated. The Annesley to Woodford 'runners' or 'windcutters' then achieved optimum productivity, with the men making one return trip daily and, in many cases, the locomotive making two. They will be remembered as an object lesson in the operation of heavy mineral traffic by steam power.

A celebrated oddity remains to be described. The requirements of the milk depot at Marylebone were met by a daily train from Dorrington, a tiny place in deepest Shropshire on the Shrewsbury and Hereford Joint line. The LNER was at pains to use its own metals as far as possible for the 'Dorrington Milk'. After reaching Banbury via Shrewsbury and Wolverhampton, the train was taken over from the GWR, leaving at 5.42 p.m. in the reverse direction for Woodford. There it reversed a second time and ran to Marylebone via Aylesbury, arriving at 8.20 p.m. The engine had worked down via Aylesbury with the empties, leaving Marylebone at 2.9 p.m., changing direction at Woodford and arriving at Banbury at 4.50 p.m. On Sundays the empty train ran via Wycombe and Woodford. At Ashendon Junction it was within 23½ main line miles of Banbury via Aynho. However, it still proceeded via Woodford, now reversing at North Loop, all the other Woodford boxes being closed, covering 40¼ miles from Ashendon to Banbury.

Tank engines were appropriate with the reversals at Woodford, and additional water stops were therefore booked at Aylesbury going down and Great Missenden returning. Neasden had an allocation of Class L1 (later L3) tanks which appeared on the train but tender engines were also used. After nationalisation, Neasden men signed for the Western road and worked to and from Banbury by the logical route of High Wycombe, Ashendon and Aynho.

Although nationalisation simplified the working of the 'Dorrington Milk', another roundabout route was in use towards the end of the life of the Great Central line. As in 1939, three fish trains still ran daily through Woodford to the west in the summer of 1963. Trains

3V11, 4.30 p.m. from Grimsby, and 3V07, 6.5 p.m. from Hull, used the Woodford to Banbury connection. However, 3V05, the 3.30 p.m. from Hull, continued on the main line to Calvert. Here it was set back over the 1940 spur to Calvert LNE Junction on the ex-LNWR line from Bletchley to Oxford. The train was taken forward to Oxford by a fresh engine. The engine which had brought the train from the north returned over the spur and, after waiting for two down parcels trains to precede, ran back light to Woodford. The spur was used at the time for parcels and night passenger trains diverted to Marylebone due to electrification work on the line to Euston. It has been suggested that the route of 3V05 was adopted in order to justify the retention of the ex-LNWR line west of Calvert at a time when closures were rife. The detailed timings of the train south of Woodford were:

	arr. *p.m.*	*dep.* *p.m.*
Woodford	pass	8.34
	3V05	
Calvert	9. 3	9.22
	Propelled	
Calvert LNE Junction	9.30	9.48
	Light Engine	
Calvert	9.54	10.24
	Light Engine	
Woodford	11. 2	

Observers of the long intervals between the departures of lightly-loaded expresses from Marylebone were apt to conclude that the Great Central's extension to London was an expensive failure. An appreciation of the volume of goods and mineral traffic passing through Woodford in 1939 would have at least modified that conclusion. When the post-1939 traffic expansion, with its culmination in the intensive Annesley to Woodford workings, is considered, who can equate the London Extension with failure?

Source:
LNER, Great Central Section, Working Time Table for Summer 1939.

Thanks are due to John Murray (Publishers) Ltd. for permission to quote from 'Great Central Railway' by John Betjeman, published in *John Betjeman's Collected Poems.*

B8 No. 1353 was No. 5442 before the 1946 renumbering. It survived until March 1949 but never carried the British Railways prefix to its number.
AUTHOR'S COLLECTION

CHAPTER EIGHT

THE GREAT NORTHERN & GREAT EASTERN JOINT RAILWAY AND WHITEMOOR

THE Directors of the Great Eastern Railway had a long-standing ambition to obtain independent access to the Yorkshire coalfield. As early as 1864 they proposed a Great Eastern Northern Junction Railway. This was to have diverged from the Cambridge to St Ives line at Long Stanton to proceed north via Ramsey, Peterborough, Bourne, Sleaford, Lincoln and Gainsborough to Askern Junction near Doncaster. The Bill was rejected after a long Parliamentary hearing. In 1867, the Great Northern opened lines from March to Spalding and Doncaster to Gainsborough, both of which were ultimately to form part of the joint railway. The GNR and GER were, however, unable to agree terms for GER running powers from March to Doncaster via the GN loop line through Boston.

An independent proposal of 1871 for a Long Stanton to Lincoln line was also stillborn despite the backing of the Manchester, Sheffield & Lincolnshire. This was the Coal Owners Associated (London) Railway, a title chosen to form the initial C.O.A.L., – yes the Victorians had discovered acronyms! In 1878 the GER proposed the Great Eastern Northern Extension Railway, again diverging from Long Stanton but this time proceeding direct to Spalding from Ramsey and crossing the Trent east of Gainsborough. In opposition, the GNR tabled a Bill for a line to close the gap between Spalding and Lincoln. Parliament, in making a judgement on these proposals, laid down the ultimate form of the line.

The Chairman of the Commons Committee said "We are not prepared to pass the line of the GE. At the same time we are of the opinion that the GE ought to have free access to the North. This on the basis of joint ownership of lines from March to Black Carr Junction with free access to other Companies north and south of Doncaster. The Committee were prepared to pass the Great Northern Bill with clauses to ensure its being made suitable for a through line to enable the GE to obtain free access to the North."

The Bill giving effect to the proposed solution was passed on 3rd July 1879. It provided for the vesting in the two Companies under joint ownership the lines from Huntingdon by St Ives, March, Spalding, Lincoln and Gainsborough to Black Carr Junction, Doncaster, with improvements to the junctions at Huntingdon and St Ives. Included in the joint Line were 51 miles of existing GNR from March to Spalding and Pyewipe, Lincoln, to Black Carr, Doncaster, and 23 miles of existing GER from Huntingdon to St Ives and Needingworth Junction, St Ives, to March. The GER paid the GNR £415,000 for the 28 miles difference, but the GNR's share of half the cost of the new line from Spalding to Lincoln was £100,000 more (£515,000).

The new construction preserved an important aspect of the existing lines at each end – the ruling gradient in the up direction was only 1 in 400 right through from Doncaster to March, making the line ideal for mineral traffic. The two 1867 portions of the route had been built to GNR standards; the station buildings at Cowbit and Finningley, for instance, were very similar. The new Spalding to Lincoln section was equipped somewhat more expensively than either company might have deemed neccesary on its own. Each country station was provided with generous platforms with four bays of ridge and furrow roofing on the main building side and a flat roof in front of the waiting shelter on the subsidiary side. It appears that neither partner was prepared to lose face when it came to agreement on the provision of facilities.

Through traffic commenced in 1882. The GNR lost revenue due to the diversion of coal destined for the GER via the new line instead of via Peterborough. The loss was estimated as £50,000 for the first five months. But Lord Colville, the GNR Chairman, said that "It was better to have the receipts of a joint line rather than have another new line competing completely". The mileage revenue from traffic passing over the line was divided equally between the two companies. Already possessing the loop line through Boston as an alternative to its main line, the GNR made little use of the new through facilities, although it retained its previous local traffic over the now joint line between Lincoln and Doncaster. It did, however, gain at least a partial income from the GER traffic. A running junction at Huntingdon was completed in 1884 but the associated western connection at St Ives from the Huntingdon line to Needingworth Junction was never built, although Great Northern maps were drawn to give the impression that through running from London to March was possible. The connection would perforce have had a somewhat circuitous route as St Ives town lay in the apex of the existing lines. The junction at Huntingdon saw little use and was eventually removed, the bare dolls on the down home signal gantries remaining as the only reminder.

The original main source of traffic was Yorkshire coal via Doncaster. From 1896, when the Lancashire, Derbyshire & East Coast Railway was opened, Nottinghamshire and Derbyshire coal reached the joint line at Pyewipe where a GER locomotive shed was built. The GER had invested in the LDECR and were rewarded with running powers. Eventually GER locomotives worked west of Pyewipe to the colliery districts. *Table 17* gives details of the weekday goods traffic in the up direction on the Lincoln-March section in 1895, before the advent of the LDECR. It appears that at least some coal, which later would have arrived via Tuxford, was brought to Pyewipe by the MSL via Retford and Sykes Junction.

TABLE 17
WEEKDAY UP GOODS TRAINS USING THE JOINT LINE SOUTH OF LINCOLN NOVEMBER 1895

GER trains unless otherwise stated.

From	*To*	*Class of train*	*No of trains*
Doncaster Mineral	Whitemoor	Coal	7
Doncaster Mineral/Decoy	Whitemoor	Goods/Coal	4
Pyewipe (ex MSL Staveley via Retford)	Whitemoor	Coal	1
Pyewipe	Whitemoor	Coal	1
Pyewipe (ex MSL)	Whitemoor	Goods/Coal	1
Pyewipe (ex GNR Bradford)	Whitemoor (London)	Express Goods	1
Pyewipe (ex MSL Manchester)	Whitemoor	Express Goods	1
Doncaster Decoy	Whitemoor (London)	Express Goods	1
Doncaster Decoy	Whitemoor	Express Goods	1
Pyewipe	Whitemoor	Stopping Goods	1
Total trains			19
Pyewipe (GNR train calling at most stations between Lincoln and Sleaford)	Whitemoor	Stopping Goods	1
Total GNR trains			1

The GNR Pyewipe to Whitemoor goods shown in *Table 17* was balanced by a down empties working. In addition there were two other down GNR goods trains which used the Joint Line between Spalding and Sleaford. One took a curious route from Peterborough to Retford via Spalding, Sleaford and Barkstone East and North junctions, the other ran from New England to Colwick via Spalding and Sleaford making various intermediate calls. Also, in 1895, there were two GNR workings over the southernmost portion of the Joint Line from Huntingdon to St Ives, one classed as Mixed and the other as Goods. Both returned as Goods.

The four express goods workings of 1895 were probably handled by Class T26 'Intermediate' 2-4-0s (LNER E4) some of which were shedded at March. In the next generation of GER locomotives there was no mixed traffic class to bridge the gap between the 4ft 11in goods engines and the 7ft 0in Claud Hamiltons. Some of the latter were fitted with vacuum ejectors so that they could be used on the express goods workings from London, Spitalfields, to the north via the Joint Line, surely a unique instance of engines with driving wheels of such large diameter being specially equipped for hauling non-passenger trains.

The GER took a significant share of the workings on the LDECR and these continued after the latter had been taken over by the Great Central. Three through workings ran in each direction between Whitemoor and Kirkby and Pinxton in 1913. In each case the engine went on to Annesley for turning and servicing. There were also four return trips on the LDEC section, bringing coal to be staged at Pyewipe, which were powered by GER engines. Two of these were to Markham Junction with one each to Clowne and Creswell Colliery Junction. On the LDECR the load for GER engines was limited to 45 wagons on down truck trains (empties) and 35 wagons on up coal trains. The loaded limit was increased to 45 wagons for 'Engines of the No 1150 type', i.e. LNER J16/17, which implies that Y14s (LNER J15) were also used.

Growth of traffic generally and especially the addition of coal from the LDECR put pressure on the GER facilities at Whitemoor. At the same time exchange of traffic between the GNR and GER at Peterborough involved two marshalling operations and a trip working, in some cases to March. The newly formed LNER viewed an expansion at Whitemoor not only as a local requirement but also as a means of relieving the yards at Peterborough with consequent economies. The resultant project was the largest single undertaking completed by the LNER, the Manchester, Sheffield and Wath electrification remaining unfinished at nationalisation.

The first part of the Whitemoor scheme to be completed was the new up yard which was brought fully into use in April 1929. This was a gravity yard equipped with Frohlich retarders – hydraulic rail brakes of German design. Forty sidings with a total capacity of 3,311 wagons were served from the hump. In addition there were ten reception roads holding 80 wagons each. The new yard replaced 13 sidings holding 780 wagons at Peterborough East and a combined total of 27 sidings holding 1,420 wagons at Whitemoor and March. Of all these, only nine sidings in the old Whitemoor Coal Bank yard had been served from a hump.

The new up yard enabled coal traffic from Colwick to East Anglia, previously routed via Grantham and Peterborough, to be diverted to Whitemoor via Sleaford and the Joint Line. The number of daily goods trains to the Great Eastern section from Peterborough declined from 34 to 7 whilst the number from Whitemoor increased from 23 to 57. The Whitemoor scheme was completed with the new down mineral empties gravity yard which was in use by February 1933. Eddy current rail brakes, which had been developed by Westinghouse, were installed instead of hydraulic retarders. The new yard had a capacity of 6,158 wagons in place of the total of 2,500 wagons which was the limit of the old down flat yard. At that time, when most of the coal was carried in private wagons, sorting of empties so that wagons could be returned to particular collieries was as detailed a task as dealing with loaded trains. Although coal was the main commodity handled at Whitemoor, there was a large seasonal northbound flow of fruit and vegetables. This was dealt with in the Norwood yard at Whitemoor which was left relatively unchanged. Coal from the LMS continued to be handed over at Peterborough but the general concentration at Whitemoor enabled Peterborough East shed to be closed in 1939. Locomotive accommodation at March had been increased by the building of a new running shed, a contemporary of the down yard. The old GER shed was then used for repair work. The number of engines allocated rose from 107 in 1922 to 186 in 1935.

In 1935, all except one (the Pyewipe to Sleaford Class D goods) of the trains in *Table 18* traversed the Joint Line between Sleaford and Spalding, a total of 32 trains. This represented more than double the traffic of 1895 as individual train loads had increased. Three of the Colwick coal trains loaded to 65 wagons and there were some 60 wagon loads from Doncaster. The GER Y14/J15 0-6-0s had given way to O4s although the J17s, which always seem to appear in the scanty selection of photographs of the line, were still in evidence in the 1940s.

The emphasis on Whitemoor as a marshalling point led to an increase in coal traffic on the Cambridge main line. Sixteen O2s were built at Doncaster in 1932-4 specifically for Whitemoor to Stratford, Temple Mills, coal trains. For many years the entire series was shedded at March, working thirteen (later twelve) special diagrams for 65 wagon trains to Temple Mills. North of Cambridge, the returning empty trains could consist of up to 100 wagons.

Wartime activity in East Anglia led to an increase in use of the Joint Line from 1939. At one time fifty USA 2-8-0s were shedded at March, later the WD 'Austerity' 2-8-0s were prominent on the line. At nationalisation there were 30 at March owned by the LNER as O7s together with another 31 on loan. It has been claimed that activity at Whitemoor reached its peak in the 1950s when up to 7,000 wagons passed through the yards. Within a decade, however, the writing was on the wall, with collapsing traffic. Disuse of the yards was eventually made more absolute by the complete closure of the vital feeder route from Spalding. As with the Manchester, Sheffield and Wath electrification, no monument has been left to a major enterprise of the LNER for improving the handling of its goods traffic.

Much reference has been made to the Joint Line publications of the Great Eastern Railway Society.

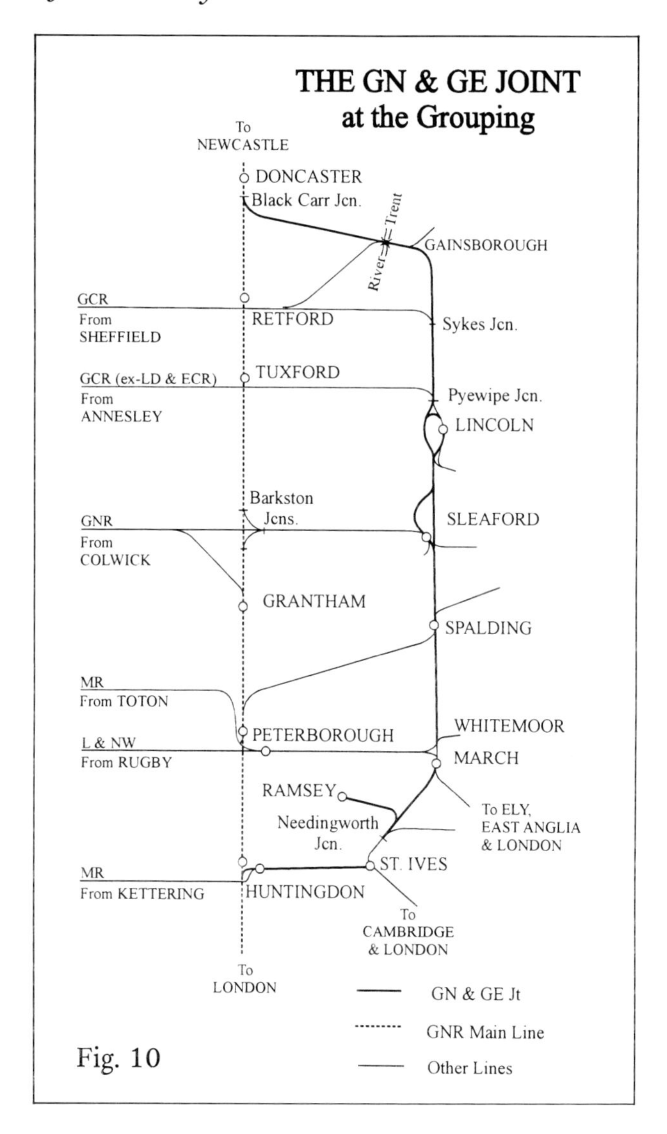

Fig. 10

TABLE 18
WEEKDAY UP GOODS TRAINS USING THE JOINT LINE SOUTH OF LINCOLN NOVEMBER 1935

From	*To*	*Class of train*	*No of trains*
Doncaster	Whitemoor	No 1 braked	1
Doncaster (ex Dringhouses)	Whitemoor	No 2 braked	1
Doncaster	Whitemoor	Class B goods	2
Doncaster (ex Dringhouses)	Whitemoor	Class B goods	2
Doncaster	Whitemoor	Class C coal	3
Doncaster (ex Wath)	Whitemoor	Class C coal	3
Doncaster	Whitemoor	Class D goods	1
Doncaster	New England	Class C coal	1
Doncaster (ex Wath)	New England	Class C coal	1
Pyewipe	Whitemoor	No 1 braked	1
Pyewipe	Whitemoor	Class B goods	1
Pyewipe	Whitemoor	Class C coal	4
Pyewipe (ex Warsop)	Whitemoor	Class C coal	3
Pyewipe (ex Mansfield)	Whitemoor	Class C coal	1
Pyewipe	Sleaford	Class D goods	1
Sleaford (ex Colwick)	Whitemoor	Class B goods	2
Sleaford (ex Colwick)	Whitemoor	Class C coal	5

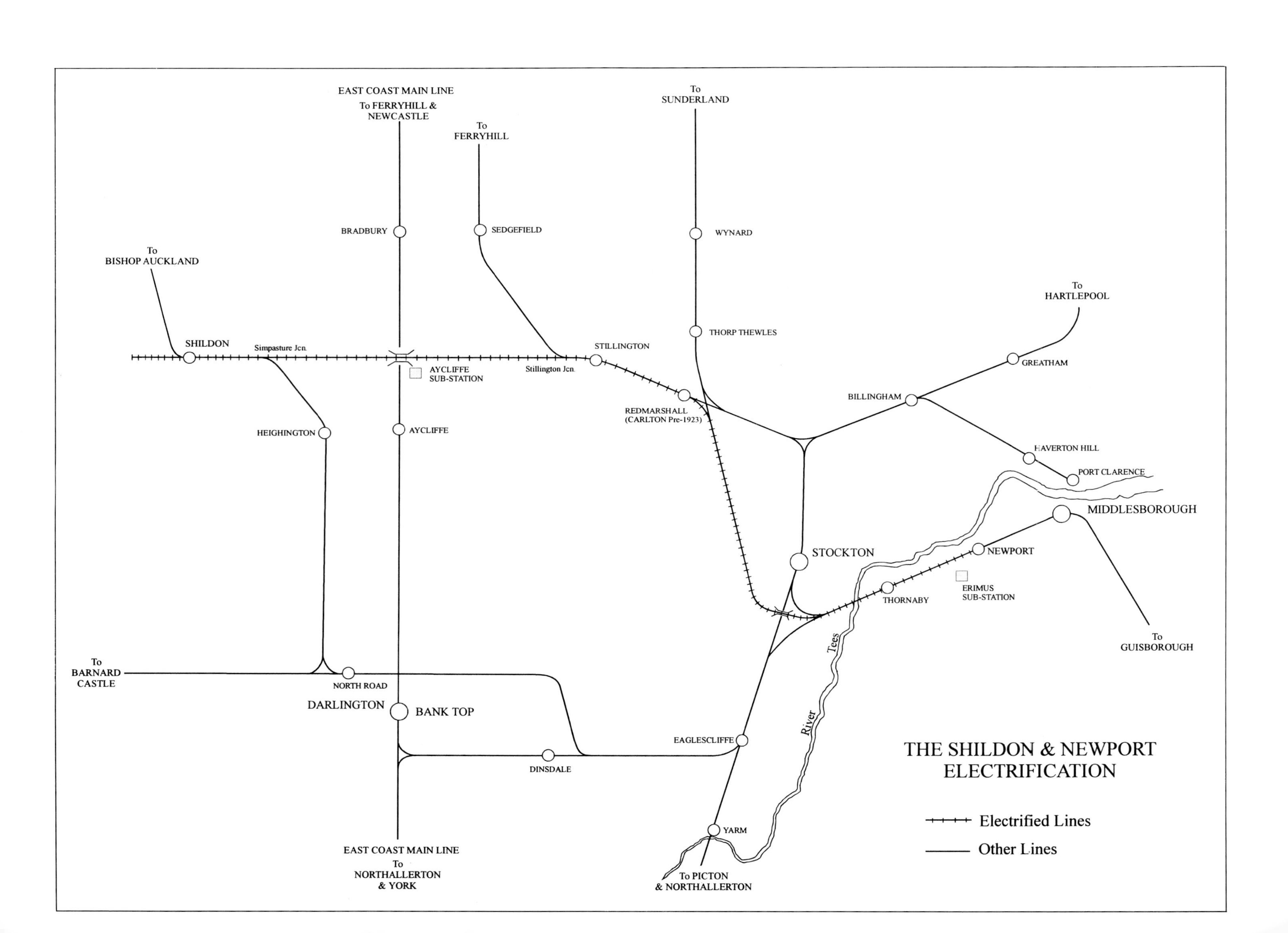
THE SHILDON & NEWPORT ELECTRIFICATION
Electrified Lines
Other Lines
EAST COAST MAIN LINE
To FERRYHILL & NEWCASTLE
To FERRYHILL
To SUNDERLAND
To BISHOP AUCKLAND
To HARTLEPOOL
BRADBURY
SEDGEFIELD
WYNARD
THORP THEWLES
SHILDON
Simpasture Jcn.
AYCLIFFE SUB-STATION
Stillington Jcn.
STILLINGTON
REDMARSHALL
(CARLTON Pre-1923)
BILLINGHAM
GREATHAM
HAVERTON HILL
PORT CLARENCE
HEIGHINGTON
AYCLIFFE
MIDDLESBOROUGH
STOCKTON
NEWPORT
ERIMUS SUB-STATION
THORNABY
To GUISBOROUGH
Tees
River
To BARNARD CASTLE
NORTH ROAD
DARLINGTON
BANK TOP
EAGLESCLIFFE
DINSDALE
YARM
EAST COAST MAIN LINE
To NORTHALLERTON & YORK
To PICTON & NORTHALLERTON

CHAPTER NINE

ELECTRIC HAULAGE OF GOODS TRAINS

Shildon roundhouse in August 1932. By that date most of the locomotives were stored out of use. PHOTOMATIC

THE LNER was the only one of the four main groups to be involved in the electric haulage of goods traffic throughout the complete 1923-1947 period. Two distinct installations were inherited from the NER and the major electrification of the Woodhead route (the Manchester, Sheffield and Wath scheme) was planned in detail, coming to late fruition under the auspices of BR.

In the period between 1900 and the grouping of 1923, the NER was very much to the forefront among British railways in the planning and implementation of electrification schemes. The North Tyneside suburban lines were electrified as early as 1904 and it was probably only the incidence of grouping that prevented the carrying out of the proposed main line electrification from York to Newcastle. Two separate non-passenger carrying lines were electrified by NER. These were the short branch to the Quayside at Newcastle and the mineral line, 18 miles in length, from Shildon to Newport.

The Newcastle Quayside branch descended from the Trafalgar Yard at Manors for about ¾ mile to the Quayside where it connected with the lines of the Newcastle Corporation. It described a semi-circle through tunnels and cuttings on a gradient varying from 1 in 30 to 1 in 27. It had been opened as early as 1st June 1870 but there had been continuing difficulties with operation by steam locomotives. When the North Tyneside suburban scheme was under consideration it was also decided to electrify the Quayside branch, not so much a prototype for goods lines generally but as a means of overcoming the local operating difficulties. Power was supplied at 600v DC. There was insufficient clearance in tunnels for overhead equipment so a third rail was used on the major portion of the branch, changing to overhead collection on the approaches to the yards at the end.

Electric working commenced on 5th June 1905, two locomotives having been purchased from the British Thomson-Houston Co. who supplied the electrical equipment. The frames and bodies were sub-contracted to Brush Electrical Engineering Co. The contract price was £4,730 for the pair and the specification required the ability to start a load of 150 tons on the 1 in 27 grade and haul it at 4½ mph. On level track the corresponding figures were 300 tons and 14 mph. The Westinghouse brake and air sanding were fitted. In later notation the locomotives would be classified as Bo-Bo, but the NER described them as 0-4+4-0. Each axle was driven by a motor of 160 hp one hour rating.

Electric locomotive No. 11 heading a Shildon to Newport coal train near Simpasture Junction in May 1923. PHOTOMATIC

The branch was operated under the regulations for 'one engine in steam' (or, in this instance, should it have been 'one electric in sparks'?). In practice, the regulations were not complied with fully. A steam shunting engine was taken down the incline by the first morning train and brought back in the evening. The simple train staff was retained on the electric locomotive. The crew of the shunting engine had no authority, therefore, to venture on to the incline unless hauled by the electric locomotive. Due to limitations in rounding facilities at Quayside, the normal procedure for working steep inclines (to have the locomotive at the lower end of the train) was not adhered to in this instance. The train was propelled down the incline and hauled back. Protection against runaway was provided by a 20 ton brake van fitted with sanding apparatus which was always at the lower end; wagon brakes were also pinned down as necessary on descending trains.

Changeover from overhead to third rail and vice-versa was made manually while running. The locomotives were provided with a knife switch, initially unprotected, to select the supply connection from pantograph or shoes. Nowadays, such a switch would arouse the interest of the Health and Safety Executive. The pantograph was retracted manually and pinned, being pulled down by a rod protruding through the roof. The overlaps between third rail and overhead were short, as were the gaps between overhead and the tunnel mouths. It was the duty of the driver's 'helper' to perform the changeover. A 'helper' was required in any case as there was no deadman's provision in the driving controls. The lack of protection in the electrical equipment is illustrated by an accident which occurred to a driver on 27th February 1933. The connections from the pick-up shoes on each side were completed through pairs of two copper strips acting as fuses. These had been renewed using one strip only in each pair. On a run from Quayside with eleven wagons and a brake van, the two fuses on one side blew with the train in the tunnel. The driver started to renew the fuse strips by the light of the flare lamp. The strips were secured to studs by nuts. On connecting the first strip, there was a flash, burning the driver's face and scorching his rubber gloves. He had left the controls open and had not drawn the main knife switch before commencing the repair.

The locomotives were numbered 1 and 2 by the NER. Neglecting a temporary re-numbering of No. 1 as 4075 in 1944, the original numbers were retained until they became 6480/1 under the 1946 scheme. With the advent of BR's 20000 series for electric locomotives, they became Nos. 26500/1 in 1948. In 1961, No. 26500 was repainted in NER lined green livery, followed by No. 26501 in 1962, a fine tribute to what was then some 56 years of unbroken service. Finally, in 1964, a diesel shunter took over the duty. The last electric working was on 29th February 1964 and the locomotives were then withdrawn. Diesel working only lasted for five years as the branch was closed completely on 16th June 1969. Fortunately, No. 26500 has been beautifully restored as NER No. 1 and is now a worthy member of the national collection at York.

The most remarkable feature of this pioneer electrification was its long survival, virtually unchanged. It spanned 59 years from 1905, in the infancy of electric traction, to 1964, well into the 25kV era. At the end, by contemporary standards, much of the equipment was archaic and some of it was downright dangerous, but it is a tribute to the original designers that it remained in use, virtually unaltered, for so long.

The Shildon to Newport electrification was an altogether more ambitious undertaking than the Newcastle Quayside line. In technology and operation it owed little to the latter. In 1910 Vincent Raven became Chief Mechanical Engineer of the NER. He was a keen protagonist of railway electrification. Within one year, Messer Merz & McLellan had been appointed consulting engineers to the NER to report upon the feasibility of main line electrification. In

When this picture was taken in August 1923, locomotive No. 4 had just crossed over the East Coast main line at Aycliffe with a coal train from Shildon to Newport. PHOTOMATIC

No. 26500 was supplied in 1905 for working the Newcastle Quayside branch. It is seen at South Gosforth depot on 19th May 1964, restored to NER green livery. P. H. GROOM

An early view of No. 9 at Shildon. AUTHOR'S COLLECTION

1913, the Shildon to Newport line was chosen for a full-scale trial of a system which would be suitable for application to the main line. Coal traffic was concentrated at Shildon for a haul of 18 miles to the Erimus yard at Newport, between Thornaby and Middlesbrough. It might be thought that concentrating wagons for such a short haul was uneconomic, but the County Durham coal industry was fragmented into many small pits with low individual outputs. The route was one where electric working might show its maximum advantage. The longer preparation, turn-round and disposal times required by steam locomotives became more significant for short journeys. It was envisaged that one electric locomotive would make two return trips per shift (then of ten hours) and, double manned, four return trips per day.

Ten electric locomotives were ordered, seventeen steam locomotives being replaced. It could be expected that eight locomotives would typically be available for duty, with one at works and another under local repair or maintenance, so up to 32 trips per day could have been worked. On the loadings that were envisaged initially, some 650 tons of coal could be carried by one train, so the capacity of the system would have been assessed at about 20,000 tons per day. This was a valid provision for the levels of traffic in 1913, but changing circumstances were to ensure that the electrified line was never operated at its full traffic density.

A sketch map of the route is shown in *Fig. 11*. From Simpasture Junction, where the route diverged from the Shildon to Darlington line, to Stillington Junction and again from Redmarshall to Bowesfield Junction the lines were used for goods and mineral traffic. Between Stillington and Redmarshall there were four roads, with one pair electrified. The electric trains were therefore largely isolated from passenger traffic, making it an ideal route for a pioneering installation.

Gradients were generally falling throughout from Shildon to Newport with a steepest inclination of 1 in 103 and an average of about 1 in 250. At Newport, the laden and empties mineral yards to the west of the course of the River Tees were known as the Erimus yards; to the east were the Newport goods yards.

Power was supplied by overhead conductors at 1,500v DC. This was the system recommended by Merz & McLellan based on practice in the USA. As late as 1951, the British Transport Commission still recognised it as a standard for new electrification projects, but by 1956, 25kV 50Hz, then with 6.25kV for sections with limited clearances, was accepted for the future. The initial York to Newcastle proposals actually included a change from overhead to third rail in the country sections, still at 1,500v DC, but this was soon deleted, no doubt to the relief of the contemporary platelayers.

Two sub-stations equipped with rotary converters supplied the overhead system. The choice of their locations, at Aycliffe and Erimus, is interesting. The Aycliffe sub-station was adjacent to the point where the route crossed over the East Coast main line, It could have been readily extended to supply the projected York to Newcastle electrification. The Erimus sub-station was practically at the end of the route but was well placed to supply other mineral lines feeding the Newport yards if they were later electrified. The section switches for isolating portions of the overhead lines were operated by signalmen locally, acting on instructions issued by a Control Office at Newport. The switches were operated by means of standard signal lever frames, usually housed in annexes to existing signal boxes.

Locomotive No. 10 in LNER black livery. AUTHOR'S COLLECTION

The locomotives were constructed by the NER at Darlington works with electrical equipment supplied by Siemens Bros. They were of the Bo-Bo type, classified by the NER and LNER as 0-4+4-0. Each axle was driven by a 275 hp nose suspended motor via a reduction gear ratio of 4:5:1. The drawgear was contained on the bogies, necessitating an intermediate coupling between them. A large central cab 16ft 5in long, had driving positions at the two right-hand corners. The cab also contained two blowers for traction motor cooling and the air brake compressor. Air was also used for sanding and for raising the pantograph. In the exact centre of the locomotive was a massive vertical casting housing the screwgear for the handbrake. The concept of separate driving compartments had not yet evolved and the cab must have been very noisy when the locomotive was in motion.

The sloping end compartments housed the control contractors and resistances. The main air reservoirs extended across the outer tops of the compartments, determining the radius of the curved ends. Although only three-link couplings were fitted and there was no provision for multiple working, brake coupling hoses were provided, presumably for use when towing a failed locomotive.

Part of the route was opened for electric working on 1st July 1915 but electrification was not completed throughout until 10th January 1916. By 1917, the line was operating at about one third of full capacity and this level of traffic was maintained until 1920. From then, traffic fell away due to strikes and eventual trade depression. Despite this, the maximum weight for loaded trains was increased from, 1,000 to 1,400 tons in November 1922. Mineral trains were not included in the NER's WTTs. Instead each twenty-four hours' workings were decided on the previous day in accordance with immediate requirements. So detailed information on traffic levels is scant, but K. Hoole (*The Electric Locomotives of the North Eastern Railway*) quotes an average of 62 return trips per week in 1917. In November 1928 only 26 return trips were made in one week. By 1933, expenditure was required on the overhead system and increases in charges for the supply of electricity were forecast when the contracts became due for renewal. In 1913, the estimated ton mileage for the line was 52 million. This had decreased to 7 million by 1930. Not surprisingly, it was decided to revert to steam traction. The decline of the Teeside steel industry and of coal exports had sealed the fate of a technically successful system. The last electric train ran on 31st December 1934 and the locomotives were then stored.

The Erimus and Newport yards were by then also operating at a fraction of their full capacity. In 1936, the LNER designated the whole complex as Newport, and the name Erimus, as with Severus at York an indication of the NER's love of Latin, disappeared. The 1955 Modernisation Plan included a comprehensive rebuilding of the site as Tees Yard, including a completely new Thornaby Motive Power Depot. Tees Yard opened in 1963 when the final decline of goods and mineral traffic was already evident. Like the electrification, the yard never achieved its full potential.

Long before the end of electric working it was apparent that some, at least, of the locomotives were surplus to requirements. In 1928, Gresley proposed the conversion of one locomotive to diesel-electric propulsion, with the

1500v DC electrification on the 1 in 48 Worsborough bank. D. L. WILKINSON

capability of working coal traffic from New England to Ferme Park. On 26th July 1928, the Locomotive Committee approved an estimate from the English Electric Co. of £10,751 for supply to Gresley's specification, including a 1,000 hp diesel engine to be obtained from William Beardmore & Co. Ltd. Including £1,000 for structural costs, the Committee resolved that the £11,571 be charged to Locomotive Renewals for 1929, 'with a view to experience being gained, in a comparatively short time, which should indicate whether, and to what extent, this type of traction might be made use of to advantage'.

On 3rd January 1929, the Committee learnt that the English Electric Co. was not prepared to guarantee an economy as low as that first offered, the saving being reduced from £1,142 to £738 per annum. A vacuum exhauster was also required, costing an extra £334.12.0 An order to the English Electric Co. for £10,905.12.0 was authorised and the total estimate was amended to £12,000. Then, on 1st August 1929, English Electric stated that they were unable to carry out the contract, 'Messrs William Beardmore & Co. Ltd having intimated that they cannot supply a diesel engine of the size and type required'.

It is probable that weight considerations forced Beardmore to withdraw. As built, the locomotives had a total weight of 74 tons 8 cwt, of which 24 tons 4 cwt was electrical equipment. A weight limit of 90 tons was specified for the conversion. The increase might not have been sufficient to permit the use of a diesel of the specified power, which in any case would have been unable to meet the full rating of the traction motors. The cancellation was unfortunate; with the rest of the locomotives eventually becoming redundant. The conversion of the whole class might have followed initial success and invaluable operating experience would have been gained.

In 1941/2, one locomotive was modified at Doncaster for use as a banker on the Manchester, Sheffield and Wath route. Steel buffer beams and extra sandboxes were fitted. The one hour rating was increased from 1,100 hp to 1,256 hp, presumably by improvement of the traction motor cooling system. The intended conversion of the remainder of the class was not carried out. After further storage, the modified locomotive was used from 1949 to 1960 for shunting Liverpool Street–Shenfield stock at Ilford car sheds; it never saw service on the MSW system. The remaining nine locomotives, after 15 years in store, were withdrawn in 1950, one still bearing 'North Eastern' lettering and its original brass number plates.

The MSW (Manchester, Sheffield, Wath) electrification was an altogether more ambitious undertaking. The Great Central route across the Pennines, through the twin bores of the old Woodhead tunnels, carried a very heavy goods and mineral traffic. The general flow of loaded mineral trains was westbound. Between Sheffield and the summit at Dunford Bridge the line rose for 19 miles with a gradient averaging about 1 in 130. The climb included 5 unbroken miles at 1 in 120. Eastbound from Manchester, there were 22 miles of climbing. Gradients included 7 miles of 1 in 100 and 1 in 117 from Dinting to Woodhead, followed by 1 in 201 through the 3 miles and 66 yards of the tunnel to Dunford Bridge. At Barnsley Junction, Penistone, westbound mineral traffic from the concentration yard at Wath converged. The route from Wath left the Mexborough to Barnsley line at Aldam Junction and traversed an avoiding line which included the Worsborough incline,

The pioneer EM1 Bo-Bo No. 6701 in LNER green livery with a trial train on the Manchester South Junction & Altrincham section in September or October 1941.
AUTHOR'S COLLECTION

3½ miles of 1 in 40, to join the Barnsley to Penistone line at West Silkstone Junction. Coal trains were banked throughout to Dunford Bridge. The incline required either the solitary Class U1 Garratt or two O4 2-8-0s as additional banking effort. Operation of the route by steam traction was therefore both difficult and expensive.

In LNER records, the minutes, dated 19th October 1926, of a meeting of a Committee to Consider Expenditure on Capital Account contain an early mention of what eventually became the MSW scheme. In a list of new projects, the notional sum of £3 million was listed for 'Manchester-Sheffield Main line Electrification'. In the following year, the dynamometer car was used with service trains of all categories to determine the energy requirements for electric traction. Records exist of lightly loaded expresses with B3 and D11 haulage and a stopping passenger train via Glossop headed by a C13. An O4 eastbound with empty wagons weighing 473 tons, produced a drawbar pull of 6.5 tons at 18 mph. In the same direction, an ex-GER J20, returning to March with 483 tons of empty fruit vans, recorded a pull of 7.5 tons at 11 mph. The times taken for the passage of Woodhead tunnel were 8 mins 24 secs by the O4 and 8 mins 54 secs by the J20, in both cases after a signal stop at Woodhead. The contrast, during the J20's journey, between the initial stage to Woodhead and the last lap across the fens from Spalding could hardly be greater.

The official announcement of the MSW scheme was made in November 1936. The then standard 1,500 v DC system was to be used. The profile of the route made it suitable for the application of regenerative braking. The first proposals for locomotives included express passenger and mixed traffic classes and ten banking engines, the latter to be converted from the redundant Shildon-Newport engines. As noted above, only one of the latter was actually modified and then it was used for service elsewhere. The mixed traffic classes were to be built first, and in 1939 seventy locomotives were placed on order at Doncaster with electrical equipment to be supplied by Metropolitan Vickers Electrical Co. The outbreak of war caused outdoor work on the electrification to be suspended and only one locomotive was actually built. This appeared in 1940 as LNER No 6701, a Bo-Bo with an axle loading of 22 tons, and power rating of 1,868 hp (one hour) and 1,360 hp (continuous). As was the case with the Shildon-Newport locomotives, the drawgear and buffing arrangements were contained on the bogies, an intermediate coupling being used. Limited trials were possible on the Manchester South Junction & Altrincham line, then equipped with a compatible system. In 1947, the locomotive, now No. 6000, was shipped to Holland for trials on the Nederlands State Railways, in the course of which the suspension system was modified. No. 6000 remained in Holland until 1952. On its return it was named *Tommy*, having been known as such during its time in Holland.

In July 1947 the LNER made an arrangement with the Government for the completion of the system. The cost was then estimated at £6,200,361. Further implementation took place in the days of British Railways,

Wath Electric Locomotive Depot with Class EM1 Nos. 26013, 26021 and 26026 standing outside. AUTHOR'S COLLECTION

Class EM1 No. 26054 at Gorton in August 1953.
PHOTOMATIC

Class EM2 Co-Co No. 27001 when new at Wath in March 1954. It was named Ariadne *in 1959. After withdrawal in October 1968, it ran on the Nederlands State Railways as NS 1505. It was returned to the UK in 1986 for display at the Greater Manchester Museum of Science and Industry.*
PHOTOMATIC

but as it was an LNER-designed project its story is briefly recounted here.

When work was resumed after the war, the condition of the Woodhead tunnels was found to have deteriorated seriously. There was no option but to bore a new double line tunnel with a consequent serious delay to the completion of the scheme. Fifty-seven 1,868 hp Bo-Bo locomotives of Class EM1 similar to No. 6000 were built at Gorton in 1950-53. They were equipped for regenerative braking in the speed range 16–55 mph. After experiments in 1955, they were modified to include rheostatic braking, available in the speed range 20–5 mph. The mixed traffic EM1 class was supplemented by the Co-Co express locomotive of Class EM2. Originally, twenty-seven EM2s were ordered in 1949, a number much greater than would be required by the MSW scheme. The power ratings were 2,760 hp (one hour) and 2,400 hp (continuous). Their top speed was 90 mph, again in excess of the 65 mph Sheffield to Manchester line speed. The quantity and specification leads to the thought that an extension of the GE section Shenfield electrification was in mind when the order was placed. In the event, only seven locomotives were actually built, entering service in 1953/4.

Electric working of goods and mineral trains from Wath to Penistone commenced on 18th August 1951 and was extended to Dunford Bridge on 4th February 1952. When the new Woodhead tunnel was completed, electric working commenced between Manchester and Penistone on 14th June 1954; the Penistone to Sheffield section followed on 20th September 1954, on which day the first public electric passenger trains ran between Sheffield and Manchester. On 3rd January 1955, the electrification was extended south of Sheffield to Rotherwood yard, between Darnall and Woodhouse, where electric haulage gave way to steam on through trains to the south. Finally, on 29th October 1965, the last extension of the network, from Sheffield to the new yard at Tinsley, was energised.

The initial loadings on the Wath/Dunford Bridge section were 850 tons westbound, with one locomotive

Class EM1 No. 26013 with a train of loose-coupled wagons.

REAL PHOTOGRAPHS

This photograph is believed to show Wath yard. H. J. STRETTON-WARD

leading and one banking, and 600 tons eastbound, with two locomotives leading to provide sufficient braking effort. It proved difficult to share equally the load of loose-coupled trains between train engine and banker, and the westbound load had to be reduced to 750 tons. In 1970, some EM1 locomotives were equipped for multiple working to enable them to handle merry-go-round coal trains from Wath to Mottram yard near Godley Junction. The ultimate destination of the trains was Fiddlers Ferry power station near Warrington. Two locomotives hauled air-braked trains of about 1,350 tons, with two additional locomotives as far as Penistone.

The MSW operation had passed its peak when the merry-go-round trains were inaugurated. The inexorable process of Derbyfication had already ensured that Sheffield/Manchester passenger services were confined to Sheffield Midland station and the Dore and Chinley line. The last weekday passenger train via Woodhead ran on 3rd January 1970. Before then, in 1968, the EM2 class locomotive had been deemed surplus to requirements and were then stored. In 1969 they were sold to the Nederland State Railways on which they worked with success until 1986, with two returning to Britain for preservation. Gradually the goods traffic over Woodhead declined in volume. In a manner reminiscent of the Shildon-Newport closure, noises were made about expenditure being required on maintenance of the overhead system. Complete closure came in 1981, the last electric trains running on 18th July. Conversion to 25kV and a relatively short extension to Doncaster would have provided an invaluable link between the east and west coast electrifications.

No. 26510 at Ilford car sheds on 27th February 1954. Originally NER No. 11, it was modified but not used for banking on the Manchester, Sheffield and Wath line. It worked as a shunter at Ilford from 1949 to 1960. A. R. GOULT

Today there is no more poignant scene of abandonment on Britain's railways than the empty track bed reaching up from Hadfield towards Woodhead. This is not the typical remnant of a little used branch line, closed with a celebratory last train and a few detonators. The route over Woodhead was a veritable artery of commerce, carrying a traffic which fully justified the post-war completion of the largest of all projects for the furtherance of the goods traffic of the LNER.

Sources:

K. Hoole, *The Electric Locomotives of the North Eastern Railway* (The Oakwood Press, 1988).

Dr G. J. Hughes, A 1929 Main Line Diesel, *The Gresley Observer No. 88* (The Gresley Society, 1989).

K. C. Appleby, *Shildon–Newport in Retrospect* (RCTS, 1990).

APPENDIX 1

CLASSIFICATION OF LNER GOODS TRAINS

No. 1 Express Goods. Vacuum piped throughout. Number of fully braked vehicles shown in table below. Not more than two piped only vehicles to be coupled together. Brake vans to be fully braked. Average speed 50 mph. [BR Class C]

No. 2 Express Goods. Number of fully braked vehicles connected to the engine by vacuum brake pipe shown in table below. Remainder of load may be loose-coupled. Average speed 40 mph. [BR Class D]

No. 3 Express Goods (Braked). Number of fully braked vehicles connected to the engine by vacuum brake pipe shown in table below. Remainder of load may be loose-coupled, Average speed 35 mph. [BR Class E]

No. 3 Express Goods (Unbraked). Maximum load, 45 loaded or 50 empty unbraked wagons. 2 or 3 wagons in front to be fully fitted if possible. Average speed 35 mph. [BR Class E]

	Number of Wagons		
Total in train		*Number Full Braked*	
	No. 1	*No. 2*	*No. 3 (Braked)*
12	9	2	–
18	–	–	0
19	–	–	1
20	15	5	–
24	18	–	–
27	–	8	2
30	23	9	–
40	31	13	6
48	38	16	9
60	47	20	12
68	–	–	16
75	–	–	20

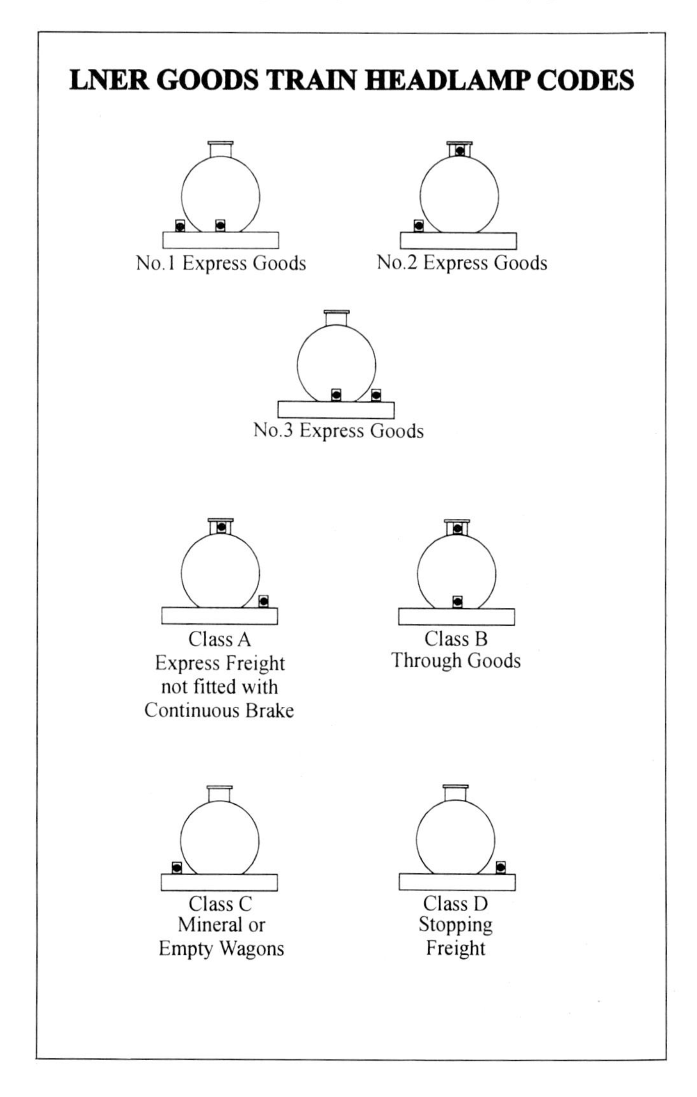